Montclair & Environs 21st Century Chronicles

*To Gene & Scott,
Thank for your help*

Montclair & Environs
21st Century Chronicles

By Philip M. Read

Philip M. Read

Foreword by Yogi Berra

Text and photographs copyright © 2002-2009 The Star-Ledger.
All rights reserved. Reprinted with permission
ISBN 978-0-557-08124-0

FOREWORD

Reading the paper every day is my daily habit. Anything that's newsworthy, that's what I read. What's happening in sports and what's happening in my town, Montclair, that's always news to me.

The Ledger is the first thing I read every morning. Sure, newspapers are old-time media, but it's still a lifeline for what is going on - especially local news. Hopefully, it stays around a long time because I'd get lost without it."

-- Yogi Berra, Yankee great

INTRODUCTION

Stop to talk to anyone, and there's a fascinating story to be heard. Each time, you walk away truly amazed, saying, "Life is stranger than fiction."

"Montclair & Environs, 21st Century Chronicles" is all about those discoveries, ones I've encountered in this first decade of the new century. It is really a travelogue, where the past crosses into the present and reveals those little truths about the human existence.

Walk through the old Essex Penitentiary in its final days and eyeball the inscription "ubnjail" on the concrete wall. Step inside a Verona diner and learn that it was once run by singer Connie Francis' father. Hear a woman at a jewelry booth tell of seeing a "very skinny" Frank Sinatra sing at the old Meadowbrook Ballroom. Or visit a cookout with ham radio operators as they meet their special guest, a descendant of Fletcher Christian of "Mutiny on the Bounty" fame.

And you're only getting started.

Philip M. Read

TABLE OF CONTENTS

FOREWORD .... *I*
INTRODUCTION .... *III*

MONTCLAIR

1. LONG AFTER VISITING THE MOON, YOU CAN GO HOME AGAIN ...1
2. A PROUD SPORTS TRADITION 4
3. ONCE SHINY, NOW DUSTY & NEARLY FORGOTTEN........................8
4. THE LEGEND PLAYS ON 11
5. THE PHARMACY THAT TIME FORGOT 15
6. THIS OLD HIDING SPACE 18
7. A PORTAL TO LIVES OF BLACKS 21
8. PLAY IT AGAIN...25
9. SOMEWHERE, 'OVER THE RAINBOW'...28
10. FUNCTION OVER BEAUTY 31
11. MONTCLAIR BREWS FAIR-TRADE JAVA 35
12. MONTCLAIR REDISCOVERS THE FRONT PORCH 38
13. MONTCLAIR'S LEAST WANTED 41
14. PASTA AND SAUCE, PLEASE, AND HOLD THE CORNED BEEF 44
15. THE LAST LAP FOR A CHAMPION 47
16. OFFICERS PUT ON A BIG SMILE FOR SHOT IN HISTORY BOOKS ..51
17. FOR SALE: 5BR, 3.5BTHS, FAMOUS OCCUPANT 57
18. LITTLE HOUSE, BIG SAVINGS...61
19. AN OBAMA TIDAL WAVE 64
20. MY EVENING WITH YOGI 67
21. OH, SAY, CAN YOU HEAR?...70
22. A GRAND STAGE REVEALED..73
23. WELCOME BACK, WELLMONT 76
24. HURRY UP AND WAIT 82
25. THANK YOU AND FAREWELL, MR. GREER 85

ENVIRONS

1. CLIFTON SECTION LOVES ITS NEIGHBOR 89
2. OUT OF THIS WORLD, BUT CLOSE TO HOME 92
3. YES, IT'S TRUE: TOM CRUISE SLEPT HERE 95
4. MOMENTOS OF ACTOR EDDIE BRACKEN 98
5. IT TOOK A HOBOKEN GIRL TO STRIKE OUT
   LITTLE LEAGUE'S BAN 101
6. NOTES FROM THE UNDERGROUND 104
7. THE JOINT'S GONNA JUMP AGAIN 107
8. RUNNING ON EMPTY 110
9. MONTCLAIR: THEY LOVE IT BUT LEAVE IT 113
10. ONE LAST LOOK AT LIFE ON THE INSIDE 120
11. IT'S CIAO TIME FOR A DINER OWNER 123
12. 'AWFUL' LOT OF MEMORIES 125
13. TODAY'S SPECIAL: MEMORIES OVER EASY 128
14. THE FRIAR TUCK'S CLOSING CHAPTER 131
15. THE MEN BEHIND THE MEN BEHIND THE MASKS 135
16. TO CATCH A SPEEDING BULLET 138
17. THE BIG PICTURE IN GLEN RIDGE 141
18. HAM OPERATOR MEETS A FARAWAY VOICE 143
19. ACTRESS HOME TO FILM '70S FLICK 'GRACIE' 146

Buzz Aldrin pays a second visit in one day to his one-time house on Princeton Place in Montclair, after speaking at his elementary alma mater, the Edgemont School. Photo by Mia Song. Run date, May 27, 2005

1

LONG AFTER VISITING THE MOON, YOU CAN GO HOME AGAIN

Aldrin, pride of Montclair, waxes nostalgic on stop

Buzz Aldrin was the bow tie-wearing wizard in the school production of "The Wizard of Oz" when he last walked the stage of Montclair's Edgemont School.

Yesterday, six decades later, "Montclair's man on the moon" came home, standing by that stage not as actor but as astronaut-turned-author.

"You will remember your lives here better than I remember last week," Aldrin told the 300 pupils who, with dozens of teachers and hordes of parents, packed the auditorium like so many moon rocks.

Aldrin, 75 and wearing a "Toy Story" necktie featuring Buzz Lightyear, stopped by Montclair along a multi-state tour to promote his illustrated children's book, "Reaching for the Moon," whose pages include his boyhood home on Princeton Place.

Minutes before his scheduled 8:45 a.m. arrival, Aldrin made a surprise visit to the house, ringing the doorbell and meeting Dolores Kelly, whose substantial home alongside Montclair's Anderson Park is marked curbside by a large moon-like rock with a plaque noting Aldrin's "original home."

"I asked if I could kiss him," Kelly said. "I did" - a peck on the cheek. "This has been the most fantastic morning."

Back on Sept. 6, 1969, there were nine bands, 15 floats and 20,000 spectators when the Apollo 11 astronaut rode in an open Cadillac convertible to the screams of "Hello, Buzz!" in a mile-long motorcade that in Montclair will forever mark Buzz Aldrin Day. It was just weeks after he and Neil Armstrong had stepped off the lunar module Eagle and made their epic lunar walk.

"It's always a pleasure to return to one's hometown," he was quoted as saying on that day 36 years ago.

This day was no different.

During the morning visit, Aldrin's memories came rushing back.

He recalled his sixth-grade class picture, taken outside the school. "I was among the shortest," he said. Inside the auditorium, he reflected on how life would take him into space - "Little did I know when I was in this room, trying to play the clarinet, not very well."

Shortly after arriving, he was asked if he remembered his kindergarten classroom. "Yes, right up here. . . .We took naps on rugs."

In an old classroom, now the school library, he stood by rows of Apple computers made of blue and clear plastic and showed he's still very much technologically adept. Out came two hand-held communication devices: "They're redundant," he explained of their functions.

In the auditorium, Aldrin stood straight, blue jacket buttoned, and oh so quietly mouthed the words as the children sang: "My country 'tis of thee. Sweet land of liberty. Of thee I sing . . . "

Aldrin's talk, too, spoke of liberty. "There are people who say yes, and people who say no. The great thing about our country is we can say what we feel," he said.

He was asked about the words he spoke when he became the second person to set foot on the moon, an event witnessed by the largest television audience in history.

"Magnificent desolation," Aldrin said.

It was July 20, 1969, when Aldrin walked on the moon, just 19 minutes after Armstrong had climbed down from the lander and spoken the words, "That's one small step for man, one giant leap for mankind."

It was Jan. 20, 1930, when Edwin E. Aldrin Jr. was born in Montclair, son of an aviation pioneer and a mother whose maiden name was Moon.

He was the quiet Montclair High Class of '47 pole vaulter who went on to West Point, then the Korean War, flying 66 combat missions in a Sabre jet and shooting down two MiG-15s. He landed his doctorate at the Massachusetts Institute of Technology. He orbited the Earth with the Gemini missions and eventually logged 290 hours in space.

More recently, Aldrin, who now lives in California, authored books on the future of space travel and founded a rocket design company, Starcraft Boosters Inc.

His return to Montclair - his first in a dozen years - came on a moment's notice.

"All abuzz," Adunni Slackman Anderson, Edgemont's principal, said of the school's mood just hours after learning Tuesday of the impromptu visit.

Moments before Aldrin's arrival, parent Lisa Kyono came rushing through the school's front doors, sporting a 4-inch round button with a picture of the Apollo 11 crew and the words "America Salutes 1st Men on the Moon."

She was 7 when the two astronauts landed. When asked when she got the button, Kyono said: "That day. I've been carting this around for 36 years."

Inside the auditorium, fifth-grader Emma Gilruth was waving a banner reading "Montclair's Man on the Moon."

"Buzz Aldrin gave it to my grandfather," she said.

Her grandfather had played football with Aldrin at Montclair High, she said. By the time of the welcome-home parade in September 1969, he was a police officer, and he was alongside the motorcade when the gift was made, she said.

Before leaving town, Aldrin - escorted by his HarperCollins publicist and illustrator Wendell Minor - stopped again at his boyhood home.

"We planted this dogwood," he said while walking toward the side of the house. Then he pointed to the ragged-edge brick of the chimney, which he said he used to climb to the window of his third-floor bedroom.

"Getting down the roof was not easy," he said.

Larry Doby, shown with his daughter Susan Robinson, is part of a great baseball tradition in Montclair. Photo by Mia Song. Run date, April 6, 2003.

2

A PROUD SPORTS TRADITION
More to Montclair than meets the ball

They all know Yogi Berra, the catcher with more World Series rings than any man in baseball history.

But there's more to Montclair's connection to big-league baseball than Yankee pinstripes.

Larry Doby, the Cleveland Indian who in 1947 broke the color barrier in the American League, still lives there, a transplant from Paterson who makes time for a little golf. "About a 10 handicap," he says. "That's not bad."

Earl Williams, the National League's rookie of the year with the Atlanta Braves in 1971, isn't around anymore, but he's close enough - in Somerset - and still visits his mom regularly. His favorite haunt: "My kitchen," says Dolores "Bobby" Reilly, Earl's mother.

"There's a really good heritage here," said David Kaplan of the Yogi Berra Museum and Learning Center, on the campus of Montclair State University.

Dale Berra, Yogi's son, spent a decade in the majors, establishing a big-league record by reaching base seven times on catchers' interference and for a time holding the record for father-son home runs (407) with his famous Dad.

"Montclair has always been my home. Even when I played in Pittsburgh (for the Pirates), I always called Montclair home," said the younger Berra from his office at the museum.

So this is Montclair's connection to baseball.

Waite "Schoolboy" Hoyt, who became a mainstay for six Yankee pennants in the 1920s, is said to have once lived at 229 Upper Mountain Ave. George "Mule" Haas, who ended his career with the Philadelphia Athletics in 1938, slept at 109 Valley Road. Billy "The Bull" Johnson - a third baseman who led the Yankees with eight runs in the '47 World Series, twice as many as runner-up Joe DiMaggio - grew up at 73 Forest St.

The street addresses are recalled with a snap by Morris Walensky, who was a mail carrier in Montclair for more than half a century and a connoisseur of local baseball legends. Now 85 and living in Toms River, he recalls Johnson's early days on "the sandlots of Montclair."

It was a league for 12- to 15-year-olds, and Johnson was the star pitcher. "We won 39 out of 40 games. He pitched 39," said Walensky, who to this day writes to his "best friend" in Augusta, Ga.

For some, there are a lot of homecomings.

Earl Williams says he's been to practically all his Montclair High Class of 1965 reunions and bumps into people he knows at the local Pathmark during regular visits to his mom's place, on Draper Terrace, where he grew up.

"I went to school with a lot of exceptional players," says Williams, making note of a Joe Walsh. "The guy who played guitar for the Eagles," he adds with a laugh.

Williams is good friends with Larry Doby and Hank Aaron, who is the only Brave besides himself to hit a ball into the upper deck in the now-demolished Fulton County Stadium in Atlanta. "We bonded on a closer level, and I'd say the same thing about Larry Doby. That's what category of friendship it is."

Doby, he says, has shared with him the stories of those early days, when Cleveland Indians president Bill Veeck signed Doby, saying, "I am not interested in the color of his skin. I'm looking for good ballplayers."

A picture of Veeck today sits atop the large-screen television in Doby's home, where he has lived since 1959. Atop his desk is his now-retired number "14" jersey. There's the black-and-white picture of a catch in a 1954 game. There are pillows - and a throw - with the emblem of the Cleveland Indians about. There's the "key to the city" from Camden, S.C., his birthplace.

And perhaps most important, his youngest daughter, Susan Robinson, a Montclair High Class of 1980 grad and a teacher's aide at the Nishuane School just down the street. She's been living with her dad since her mother, Helyn -Doby's high school sweetheart at Paterson's Eastside High - died in 2001.

She knows of the prejudice her father quietly endured. He was the recipient of what one sports writer called the "iceberg act" in the dugout. He could "read disdain in his teammates' eyes" before a thaw began to settle in.

"He took it all in," she said of her father. "To endure all that. . . . From talking to him, you'd never know, he's very humble."

The man described in 1949 as "the shy guy who became brash at bat" - who batted .318 in the 1948 World Series and who now is enshrined in baseball's Hall of Fame - still appears to be a man of few words.

Daughter Susan - he has four other grown children nearby - notes that Doby was manager of the Chicago White Sox in 1978. "You have a good memory, Sue," he says.

When asked how the season went, Doby says: "Not good. Not good," and smiles. For the record, the White Sox won 37 and lost 50 in the 87 games he managed.

Being the youngest, Susan says, she missed out on a lot of her dad's career. "I saw him manage and coach. When I was growing up, I'd always travel with my mom to the places where he was, and that's how I realized what a great person he is."

Just down the street at the Nishuane Park baseball diamond last week, Jim Lauterhahn, the junior varsity coach from Immaculate Conception High School, was pitching to young batters. He was keenly aware of Doby's Montclair roots. Asked if his boys knew, he said: "Probably not, and that's probably my fault."

It is difficult enough keeping them abreast of the latest baseball doings, he said. "To get them into history is a little tough."

That means they probably didn't know that Chris Chambliss, who won the American League Rookie of the Year Award in 1971, was once an intern for Montclair's Department of Parks, Recreation and Cultural Affairs.

He was going to Montclair State in the off-season and organized recreation activities around 1981, as best as Lonnie Brandon, then superintendent of park services, remembers.

"Very personable," Brandon said of his one-time intern. "The only time I've seen him since is on television."

As for Yogi, he remains perhaps Montclair's most famous big-league face. He, like Doby, has been in Montclair for more than 40 years. "My wife picked it out," he said when asked how he wound up in town.

In the mornings, he's known to pick up his paper and coffee at Henry's in nearby Verona. He works out in the gym at South Mountain Arena in West Orange. "I don't lift what they lift," he says of the weights.

Still, he's fond of the in-Montclair attractions.

"It looks like restaurant row on Bloomfield Avenue," he says. And he knows he's an item.

"They all know me as Yogi. They all say 'Hi.'"

Vincent Valenti, left, Class of '57, pulls out the trophy awarded for the state football championship to Montclair High in 1956, as Bill Kennedy, Class of '58, looks on. Photo by Mitsu Yasukawa. Run date, Nov. 28, 2006.

3

ONCE SHINY, NOW DUSTY & NEARLY FORGOTTEN

Reclaiming Montclair's athletic glory

The portraits of Montclair High's football greats - coaches Clary Anderson and Angelo "Butch" Fortunato - are tucked away largely out of view in a hallway leading to Principal Mel Katz's office.

But for all the school's athletic glory, there's little more. No rows of shiny trophies in the lobby's glass display cases. No plaques paying homage to the greatest running back of '56.

Those, it turns out, had been relegated to "The Pit," a basement burial ground of glory days past, a testament to the fleeting nature of fame.

There, literally on the scrap heap of history, is the statue of a "victory" lady holding high a gold wreath crown, honoring the state champions in 1925's track and field events. "Won by Montclair High School" reads the fading inscription.

Sitting nearby is a large silver cup, perhaps the oldest, for Montclair High's athletic honors in the "Interscholastic Relay Race" of April 22,

1901, its shine long since gone.

"There must have been 500 of them," Bill Kennedy, a MHS alum from '58 and semi-retired sportswriter, said of the find.

There, with '57 alum Vincent Valenti, he first ventured into "The Pit" last summer in the hopes of seeing them prettied up and displayed at a new fieldhouse to be built largely from the generosity of the family of a celebrated halfback in the 1940 season, Robert "Fuzzy" Furlong.

"If we hadn't come down here, they would probably have been thrown out in a couple of years," Valenti said after he ventured into the locked cavern of Montclair High this month after a planning session for next year's 50th reunion.

To Valenti, it's personal.

In the autumn of 1956, the senior Mountie halfback was in the thick of the kind of championship season that becomes the stuff of Hollywood legend.

"We were undefeated all three years we were there. We beat Clifton. We beat Bloomfield," he said. "Until they met us, they were undefeated."

Today, his team's once mighty trophy - personally grasped by the hands of Anderson and Fortunato themselves back on Dec. 6, 1956 - could be mistaken for junk.

The glittering figurines of the quarterback, left arm extended as a scope for the grand right-hand pass to come, and the scorer, arms raised as he holds the victorious leather-skin football in the end zone, are gone. Its sizable base is broken.

It is among the dust-layered trophies Kennedy and Valenti sorted by decades and that are now standing atop what looks like a long elevated walkway. "It was dirty," Kennedy said of the task, seen as a first step to finding donors to fund their repair.

To be sure, Montclair High does show off sports trophies in display cases outside the gym and in the cafeteria, but they're all of recent vintage.

"Just because of the sheer number of the trophies and plaques we've accumulated, it's been difficult," said John Porcelli, the assistant principal of athletics and student activities.

Steven Timko, executive director of the New Jersey Interscholastic Athletic Association, said space is an issue. "The more success you have, the harder it is to fit all the trophies in," Timko said.

Mindful of that, the NJIAA for this first time this year has re-designed its championship trophy. The base is removable. The figurine of the athlete is mounted on the side, rather than teetering on the top. "If you can't fit them in your trophy case, you have the ability to unscrew them and mount them on the wall," he said.

The fenced-in "pit" at Montclair High School contains sports mementos not yet on anyone's radar, such as gray tins of old 16-mm film reels with footage from the Montclair-Nutley game of 1949, among others. Perhaps one day, Kennedy said, some could be digitally remastered.

"The Fifties, most of those are gone. '53. '54. '55. '56," Valenti rattled off.

"Butch (Fortunato) use to loan them to somebody," Kennedy said of the films, "and I don't know, they never came back."

Amid the relics is evidence of Montclair's sports-present. A costume head of Montclair's mascot, the Bulldog; four-shelf carts holding 16 basketballs apiece; even blue-and-white pompons.

There, too, are the often-spotted large orange tubs of Gatorade, a relative newcomer to the gridiron.

Beneath the elevated platform is a single table, what might be called the island of misfit trophies.

"These are just pieces," Kennedy said. Some barely recognizable. Some might, just might, be matched up with others, even - maybe - made whole again.

For Kennedy and Valenti's efforts, Porcelli has nothing but praise.

"It's terrific," he said. "One of the neat things about Montclair is there's a very rich tradition athletically."

To Kennedy, who played baseball under Clary and basketball under Fortunato and today is chairing the Class of '58 reunion committee, the famed coaches instilled an inner gift, beyond the glow of the cast-metal figure of a muscular athlete.

"Two great men in my opinion and two great men whose lessons in life still influence my life," Kennedy said. "That may sound corny. That may sound high-school-ist."

The lessons? "Athletic standards go right along with academic standards," Kennedy said. "(They) certainly had us pointed in that direction. Both Clary and Butch."

The living room of this Montclair home was once the piano lounge of famed composer Herman Hupfeld, who penned such classics as "As Time Goes By." "It's built for light. There's no doubt about that," said owner Maribeth Vollen. Photo by Jon Naso. Run date, Nov. 24, 2002.

4

THE LEGEND PLAYS ON

As time goes by, estate still exudes lyricist's mystique

This was Herman Hupfeld's at-home piano lounge.

The inset floor outlet that powered the light for the lyricist's Steinway is still there. So, too, are the hand-painted musical notes, seen on the beams of the vaulted ceiling.

Then there are the shadows - oh, those shadows - so reminiscent of the scenes in "Casablanca," which took 1943's Oscar for best picture and propelled Hupfeld's "As Time Goes By" into the select field of American standards.

"It's built for light. There's no doubt about that. The shadows," says Maribeth Vollen, the estate's current resident. The words "Play It Sam" can be heard off a CD soundtrack playing near her art deco fireplace, illuminated as the setting sun's light moves across the black casement windows on Montclair's Park Street.

Just like in "Casablanca."

Vollen is moving ("It's time," she says). But the folklore remains, the stories told only by those who live in - or near - such places as Hupfeld's, a stucco home built for him in 1935 just a short walk from Montclair's Watchung Plaza.

When Vollen purchased the house in 1996, she heard stories passed down from generation to generation, not among relatives but among neighbors. "I've heard the myths of the house," she said, such as the time limos stretched down Park Street to the corner of Gordonhurst Avenue when Hupfeld threw parties said to attract the likes of Bing Crosby and Mae West.

Some things about Hupfeld might indeed be myth.

Years ago, a piano at the old Robin Hood Inn in nearby Clifton sported a brass plaque saying Hupfeld wrote "As Time Goes By" on that spot.

"He did sit at the bar at the Robin Hood Inn," Jennifer Wells, daughter of onetime part-owner Francis "Jake" Jacobs, said of Hupfeld. "A lot was exaggerated."

But William McElroy - whose mother-in-law, Ruth Buttel, grew up at the inn - swears by it, noting that Hupfeld even played the piano at her wedding.

"That's what she said," said McElroy, who is general manager of Montclair's Mount Hebron Cemetery and has another connection to the Hupfeld name.

Hupfeld is buried there, next to his mother, Fredericka, who outlived her son by six years.

As for Hupfeld's actual piano, that was apparently sold years ago.

David Conrad, an attorney who has lived in Montclair since 1930, recalls responding to an advertisement that the piano was for sale and went to Park Street to look it over.

"I played a few notes on it, a beautiful sound," he said of a piano he figured dated to the late '20s. "People who know their pianos know their vintage like people know their wine."

But there was one thing Conrad didn't particularly like about it. "Somebody had painted it with a white enamel," Conrad said.

In the end, Conrad learned it would be expensive to restore and subsequently bid $13,000 for it. In a few days, he said, he heard a dealer had paid $20,000.

"I did sit down and play 'As Time Goes By,'" he said. "Apparently that's the piano that he composed it on."

Some recall meeting Hupfeld, who died in 1951 at the age of 57.

"I once met him," said Royal Shepard, who is Montclair's historian. The meeting place was a restaurant called the Three Crowns near the

Claridge Theater. "I was thrilled, of course," Shepard said of that day shortly after the end of World War II.

In later years, Shepard came across Hupfeld's name on a membership list of the Montclair Athletic Club, which today still features a hunting club but is a campus of private Montclair Kimberley Academy on Valley Road.

He notes another piece of trivia: Hupfeld sent sheet music of "As Time Goes By" to President Franklin Roosevelt and British Prime Minister Winston Churchill during their conference in Casablanca, which in the movie featured Humphrey Bogart as the cynical but sentimental "Rick" of Rick's Cafe Americain and Ingrid Bergman as his lost love in wartime French Morocco.

Not bad for a kid from Montclair High's Class of 1915, who during the Great War played sax in the Navy band and, according to his obituary, wound up writing the music for the Princeton fight song "Here Comes That Tiger."

Hupfeld actually penned "As Time Goes By" in 1931, for the Broadway musical "Everybody's Welcome." Then, it was sung by the popular platinum blond songstress Frances Williams. Later, it was picked up crooner Rudy Vallee.

Ann Taylor was a young girl then and living on North Fullerton Avenue, as she does today, in a home whose back yard faces Hupfeld's old place the next street over.

"I was only about 10 years old when he was getting the house built," she said of a time when she and her friends romped in the back yard. "He didn't like what we were doing, I'll tell you that."

Taylor remembers being a member of the Watchung Congregational Church, which burned down years ago but once featured Hupfeld's mother as the church organist and was the site of Hupfeld's funeral in 1951.

Much has changed in all those years.

Vollen said she's made substantial improvements to Hupfeld's old haunt, now on the market as a two-family home with an asking price of $875,000. Her real estate agent, Rhodes Van Note & Co., isn't letting the Hupfeld connection slip by. Its advertisement comes with the heading "You must remember this" and notes the home "easily reverts" to a four-bedroom, single-family dwelling.

And at an open house on Nov. 3, in that 33-by-19-foot room where Hupfeld's piano once sat, could be heard that tune, popularized for a new generation in the film "Sleepless in Seattle" starring Tom Hanks and Meg Ryan.

"Of course, we played it in the background," said agent Robin Seidon.

Little has changed at Bradner's Pharmacy. Photo by Scott Lituchy. Run date, Jan. 23, 2006

5

THE PHARMACY THAT TIME FORGOT

Apothecary from a lost era nears end in Montclair

Enter Bradner's Pharmacy, and the bell atop the door lets out a haunting ring from another era.

One of the first things to catch the eye is a towering scale with a coin slot for a penny and the tempting question: "Do You Weigh What You Should?" Take a few steps and walk behind the soda fountain and there's nine built-in containers for syrup. Cherry. Vanilla. Root Beer. Then, the containers for toppings. Walnut. Pineapple. Butterscotch.

The lettering on butterscotch has nearly vanished. "It's worn off the most," says Marcia Fusilli, the proprietor this day at a place modeled after an English apothecary and facing Montclair's Tudor-accented Watchung Plaza, near a quaint train station abutting Park Street.

Soon, a customer enters, eyeballs an Emerson AM radio, encased in Lucite and filled with tubes from the days before transistors and computer chips. "It's very nice. I think I might take that," says Arleen Zalewski of Glen Ridge.

They share some conversation - both, it turns out, have working rotary-dial phones at home - before Fusilli hand-cranks the National cash register and the sale pops up in the thin rectangular window: $42.40, with tax.

For decades, Bradner's has been frozen in time. Only a few modern intrusions have breached its front door. But after 85 years, Bradner's is coming to an end.

Posted inside the front windows are handwritten signs reading "Cosmetics," "Fragrances," and - the telling clue - "Antiques."

The fixtures, the merchandise of old, the concoctions of long-gone generations are up for sale. "Mrs. Thorton's this, Mrs. Hodgkin's that," Fusilli said of the pharmacy's pedigree.

There's a certain sadness here for Fusilli, whose late father purchased R.D. Bradner Jr.'s circa 1921 pharmacy back in 1953. "It was the grand day of the independent pharmacist," she said.

Her dad even won first prize - $100 - in a best-window contest sponsored by Delsey, the brand name for Wondersoft toilet tissue made by Kleenex. "That was a lot of money then," she said.

Since her father's death in 1967, his widow - Fusilli's mom, Helen - has kept the place going. But she's now in her 80s, and it's time to let go. The booth with the protruding sign "TELEPHONE" is still here, its swing door tripping an overhead light, but the actual phone has been gone since the 1980s, as best Fusilli can recall.

There's a basket filled with plastic measuring spoons imprinted with "Bradner's Pharmacy, PI-4-7676," the PI standing for "Pilgrim" in the days when words were routinely used for phone exchanges. It sits next to a display case of "Quality Combs by Pro-phy-lac-tic," including a No. 70 ladies' drawing comb, for 25 cents.

Remnants from the days of pharmacies old can be found behind the cabinet doors lining the shop. There's Lane's Tea, a remedy for constipation; Lydia Pinkham's sanative wash; Let's Save the Baby, for colds and coughs; and Stifel's Medicinal Soap, said to remove freckles.

"I'd like to sell it as a whole collection," said Fusilli, who actually worked the counter while a Montclair High student in the 1970s.

Asked how it all survived untouched, she said, "You didn't have a big turnover in ownership."

Stephen Brandt, executive director of the Garden State Pharmacy Owners, said independent shops such as Bradner's have been thinning out, with their numbers falling from about 1,350 a decade ago to about 650 today in New Jersey. It's a situation he attributes to the constraints of managed care rather than competition from the big chains.

Yet, hearing of Bradner's, he couldn't help but wax nostalgic about his boyhood job in a New York pharmacy decades ago, a place whose customers included actor Henry Morgan and the famous lyricist Oscar Hammerstein.

"You brought me right back to that day," he said when told of the soda fountain and the old phone booth.

As for the Fusillis, they intend to lease the store with one proviso: The original light fixtures and built-in cabinets must remain as they always have. "Otherwise, you've basically rented an empty shell. It's sort of like taking the heart out of the body. It doesn't work," Fusilli said.

She soon brings out a scrapbook.

"This is Mr. Bradner, and this is my pop," says Fusilli, pointing to one black-and-white snapshot of her father, Donald, who she said succumbed to kidney disease when she was just 6.

The book has a little advertising calendar marked "Bradner's Pharmacy" and dated 1934, as well as ad cards speaking to the special relationship people had with their pharmacists.

"As essential to your health as food" reads one.

"Choose your druggist as you would a doctor" reads another.

So far, she's had some inquiries about leasing the family store. "From tea room to candy store," she says. Some have even asked about bringing the soda fountain back into operation after decades of silence. "Whatever makes sense," she said.

Yet the little round tables that children once sat in while eating their sundaes are stored away at home, in Fusilli's basement. Asked if they were for sale, too, she said: "Maybe. I'm not sure. I'm not sure."

John Dickie's past met Cyndi Steiner's present when she tore up her Montclair house and found his toys and other vintage items. Photo by Jerry McCrea. Run date, Dec, 9, 2004.

6

THIS OLD HIDING SPACE

Montclair renovation reveals a child's stash

Cyndi Steiner has discovered that walls do talk.

Consider the finds in her just-purchased house on Montclair's Grove Street, where she has gutted three floors and discovered long-kept secrets of a boy named John Dickie.

Inside her walls, she pulled out toys marked with his name, a heavy metal cap gun, a rod with a soldier wrapped around it, a carved wooden boat and a homemade hand paddle with the penciled-in initials "J.D." and the date " '02" - as in 1902.

Those items appeared as Steiner and her brother, Karl, wearing heavy gloves and safety glasses and wielding crowbars, were busy removing the wood slats inside the old Victorian they're refurbishing.

Behind-the-wall finds are more common than some might think.

"I truly believe every house has some treasure. It's in the eyes of the beholder whether it has any value or not," said Bill Asdal of Asdal Builders LLC in Chester.

Asdal, who has been a remodeling contractor since 1976, can rattle off a laundry list of his finds: a 1732 English shilling, canes, a shotgun, knives, old scissors, a wooden canteen and - something that once perplexed him - shoes, lots of shoes.

"Old shoes. That used to be a sign of good luck," said Asdal, who has since researched the phenomenon.

"We really do look at every shovelful that comes out," he says of his archaeological pursuits on the job.

An episode of "Antiques Roadshow" once featured a 16th-century parade helmet from Milan, Italy, that was found in the rafters of an attic. It was valued at $250,000.

A spinoff, "Antiques Roadshow FYI," which will debut next year, will feature the story of a Massachusetts family that refinished an attic last redone in the 1930s.

"They used for wallboard some discarded movie lobby cards," said Judy Matthews, senior publicist for the show.

Pulled from the attic were undamaged art lobby cards from 1935's "G Men," starring James Cagney; 1937's "Internes Can't Take Money," another gangster film starring Barbara Stanwyck; and 1937's "A Star Is Born" starring Frederic March, among others.

"They just kind of laid them between the studs," she said. "They're pristine."

In the Steiner house, some items provided clear clues to the era, such as an Oct. 4, 1887, copy of the New York Herald and magazines dating from 1897 to 1903.

In all, there was a 4-foot collection of stuff stuck between the second-floor and what once was an unfinished attic.

"It went from oldest to newest," she said. "It had to have fallen for a period of about 5 years. Isn't that funny? It looked like the boy, John Dickie, threw them there to hide them from mom or something."

There's what appears to be a snuff box labeled "Maryland Club." A "Series 1901" box labeled "the Old Corner," which when opened shows the store that sold the "union-made" cigars. A bottle of "Pittsburgh Rye Whiskey." An "Earl & Williams" collar and cuff box with the notation "Chicago 1893. World's Columbia Exposition."

Also unearthed were a stout bottle of "Carter's Mucilage," an adhesive described in a trading card of the day as "The Great Stickist;" a still-working umbrella; collections of skeleton keys; and a padlock by Vassar Locks, ornamented in fine detail with the figure of a female graduate in gown and mortarboard. And - apparently not surprisingly - a shoe.

City directories at the Montclair Historical Society do offer clues to the home's one-time occupants.

There's a Henry Dickie listed as the house's occupant in 1897, noting that he was employed in the printing business at 287 Broadway in New York, a circa 1872 Second Empire office building with a cast-iron facade.

"I guess he was a commuter," said Alicia Schatteman, the society's executive director.

Other finds point to subsequent dwellers.

There's a small picture of a well-dressed man, with a notation on the back reading, "This is our father, Charlie Smith." A 1940s-era picture shows a woman and a girl wearing hats and, in the background, period automobiles.

All of these discoveries don't surprise Asdal, whose renovation projects carry more than just his signature on a contract.

"Virtually every job gets salted for the 21st century," said Asdal, who plants coins and newspaper clippings in walls of places he's building, for someone to find generations from now.

"I like to put things with dates on them," he said. "We always sign things."

And sometimes, "we write a little story," Asdal said. To be read in the future.

Historian Stacey Patton has been gathering photographs, letters and mementos for an exhibit called "Growing Up Black in Montclair." "Even though Montclair wasn't a Jim Crow town, there still was this unwritten language," said Patton, who is a project historian for the Montclair Historical Society. Photo by Noah Addis. Run date, Sept. 3, 2006.

7

A PORTAL TO LIVES OF BLACKS

Montclair exhibit shows early years

In the 1950s, a young Sandra Lang would trek to Montclair's cavernous Wellmont Theatre to catch a movie.

There were no signs reading "Colored Only" or anything like that. But they always took their seats — in the balcony. "They made the (ticket) prices lower upstairs," she said.

Asked if it was a subtle hint about the seating arrangements, Lang, who is African-American, said, "Absolutely."

The trek to the ice cream store wasn't exactly right either, said Lang, now Montclair's 4th Ward councilor. "You couldn't go in there. It was just understood."

Stacey Patton has been listening to these stories for some time now. African-Americans in Montclair, she said, could go to a restaurant, or so they thought. "Many remember being ignored," she said. Other times, they would be given paper cups instead of drinking glasses.

"Even though Montclair wasn't a Jim Crow town, there still was this unwritten language," said Patton, who as project historian for the Montclair Historical Society has been gathering photographs, letters and mementos for a new exhibit called "Growing Up Black in Montclair."

There are love letters between two Montclair teenagers in the early 1920s. An autograph book, filled with messages from old classmates from the 1930s. And there are Ronald Murphy's candid snapshots of children who stopped in his luncheonette, "Murphy's Thing," from 1966 to 1974.

"They didn't have pictures in their homes," said Murphy, the retired operations division chief for the Montclair Public Library and a photographer whose passion for images has since taken him on worldwide excursions.

So he posted the snapshots on a great big board for them to see at "Murphy's Thing."

The luncheonette was something of a flashpoint in Montclair's black history. In 1968, he said, black students walked out of Montclair High School, boycotting classes in the midst of the civil rights movement, and marched to his store.

Among those students, he said, was a young man named DeForest "Buster" Soaries, who went on to become secretary of state under Gov. Christine Whitman and is now pastor of the 4,000-member First Baptist Church of Lincoln Gardens in Somerset.

"He was one of the leaders," Murphy said.

To be sure, Murphy, like Lang and others, point to the opportunities of growing up in Montclair, with its relative affluence and tolerance.

"Doctors and lawyers and just plain people who have made something of themselves," Murphy said of what became of the black children who came to his store. "I was quite proud of them."

It's a message Patton, too, has heard. "They felt this sense of arrival," she said of the era.

To Doris Spivey, who long ago accompanied Lang to those 20-cent balcony seats, growing up black in Montclair was — in fact — a pleasant experience. But it masked something too.

"I didn't realize until I went to college that there were some pieces missing," she said. "We didn't know anything about black history. We were never exposed to that in Montclair schools. We didn't know any of that."

In the 1960s, before busing — and eventually magnet schools — brought integration to Montclair's public schools, Sandra Terry was a student caught up in a tracking system she neither liked nor accepted.

"I was kind of bored," she said of her middle-of-the-road track. "I'd see some of my Caucasian counterparts (in a higher-track class) and think, 'She's not too bright.'"

So she went to her mother, and they petitioned to get her in the top-tier. "One of my teachers went through my transcripts all the way to kindergarten and said, 'Ohhhhh. Okay.'

"Those are things that were not widely announced," she said of the subtleties of the tracking system.

Once Montclair started busing students to achieve integration, she said, the scene outside what had been the largely African-American Glenfield School was telling: limousines arriving at 2:30 p.m. to pick up white students.

To Terry, the message was clear. "Oh, this is a horrible area," she said of the mind-set. "They'd be out there with their arms crossed, thinking there was going to be some kind of attack there."

Yet in the end, she said, it all smoothed out. "It was like reverse busing. The town just flip-flopped for a couple years," she said of the bumpy start to integration. "It all worked out well. I think Montclair has just proved to be that type of town where people are intelligent enough and liberal enough to put that aside."

When the exhibits opens Tuesday for a monthlong run at Montclair's main library, there will be a sinister side: Patton's own collection of postcards.

One shows a little black girl leaning over a lemonade stand, where the price has been cut from 5 cents to 4 cents and finally to 3 cents. Her short dress is ripped up the back, revealing her behind. The heading on the card reads "There's 'barely' any business at all."

The racial caricatures — most always depicting children — were created by white people for a white audience, Patton said.

"Always flirtatious. Always harlots," she said. "This is a distortion of their humanity."

Patton said it doesn't anger her, a question she's been asked.

"I say, 'No.' This is about getting into the minds of those who created it. When you strip it of its humor, it reveals something very sinister and nasty. . . . It reinforces the image of black inferiority."

The photos and stories she has since collected, she said, will show how African-Americans sought to create a "counter-narrative" for their children's character and destiny.

"History is always about the search for truth," she said.

The anger in the black community — evidenced in hip-hop lyrics where singers refer to themselves in derogatory terms — is a result of a disconnect with the past and its hard-earned battles, she said. "They don't feel connected to anything," she said.

That's where "Growing Up Black in Montclair" will hopefully leave its mark, she said.

"We have a society that perpetuates the same image of failure. How do we get back to the old values?" Patton said.

Annette Speach, executive assistant to Montclair Township Manager Joseph Hartnett, alongside the 1913 Steinway & Sons piano. The keyboard of the 1913 piano appears on the cover of this book. Photos by Matt Rainey. Run date, Feb, 11, 2004.

8

PLAY IT AGAIN

Montclair keys up to sell out-of-tune Steinway

Stuart Oderman, the internationally acclaimed silent film pianist, once stroked its ivories to flashing images of Lillian Gish.

It is a Steinway grand piano, a Model "O" crafted in mahogany in a Hamburg factory as war clouds descended on Europe in 1913.

Now, nine decades later, the down-on-its-luck Steinway sits badly out-of-tune, just outside the offices of Montclair's manager and mayor, ready for the ultimate brush-off: a public auction, a fate normally afforded to wayward bicycles, discarded adding machines and tired old police cruisers.

"In its present condition, it's an eyesore. In the proper hands, it can be restored to a thing of beauty, an instrument of beauty," said Joseph Hartnett, Montclair's township manager.

The piano is to be auctioned off "as is" at 2 p.m. Friday in the second-floor boardroom of Montclair's municipal building, with a closely guarded starting price determined with the help of an appraiser.

The Model "O" - still made in Hamburg - is the largest of the "baby" grands, with ones manufactured between 1900 and 1913 considered early models.

They sometimes command handsome prices. A restored and rebuilt one, retailed at $48,900, was sold at a sale price of $29,900, according to GrandGrands.com. In recent days, similar ones could be found listed on eBay for anywhere from $19,995 to $99,000 for a Model O with a "Hamburg Art Case."

"Half-a-million or so would be nice," Hartnett said in jest of what Montclair's Steinway might bring in at auction.

The Steinway's latest odyssey is traced to 1997, when the public library on North Fullerton Street had to pull up stakes during a major renovation.

"Clearly a rescue mission," former manager Terry Reidy said of how it wound up in the waiting room outside his one-time office.

As Annette Speach, then as now executive assistant to the manager, recalls, she and Reidy - both piano players - thought they could have it tuned. "We figured a couple hundred dollars," she said. "We thought we'd split it and play after-hours."

When the restorer's estimate came in at several thousand dollars, she said, the idea was abandoned, and the Steinway's role as a stately looking, poorly sounding prop was cemented.

Still, it has drawn some passing stares and interest over the years, and since notice of the auction was published, a handful of phone calls to Joan Hoyt, Montclair's purchasing agent and the woman who will be conducting Friday's auction.

In recent days, she received a call from a mother looking for a Steinway for a son immersed in piano lessons.

"I said, 'Why would you want to buy this one?' Hoyt said. "Well, she went out to look at Steinways. They were quite expensive, $50,000 to $75,000 new . . . and they were flabbergasted."

What little is known of the Steinway's pre-move past can be traced to John Skillin, a librarian in the audio-visual department.

"My best memory of the piano would be of the time we were showing silent movies, and we had live accompaniment for Buster Keaton and Harry Langdon films," Skillin said. As best he can remember, that was in the 1980s.

The accompanist was Oderman, the author of "Lillian Gish: A Life on Stage and Screen." Now, 64, the self-described "last of a dying breed" lives in East Orange and recalls his stints at the Montclair library.

"I remember playing for some Lillian Gish movies," said Oderman, whose latest book profiling Jackie Coogan and 21 other stars of the silent screen is due out in a few months.

There was some doubt this week that the Steinway up for auction was actually the one Oberman played, but Skillin paid a return visit to the piano this week. "This is the one we used for silent movies, definitely," Skillin said.

Informed that Oderman is doing well, Skillin said: "I'm glad to hear he's still tickling the ivories, as they say."

How bad the Steinway sounds ("Oh God, it's horrible," Speach said.) and when the damage was inflicted ("It sounded fine," Skillin recalled.) remain open to debate. And whether the Steinway was a loaner or an outright gift to the now-piano-less library system is not entirely clear.

"They were on loan honestly," said Caroline Fannin, the library's public service division chief. But in regard to Montclair's decision to auction it off, she noted that the piano went to a "township entity."

"We didn't see reusing it here," she said of the Steinway.

That apparently is not the case with some other wayward possessions.

"We have a couple pieces up at the Van Vleck House," she said of the historic estate. "A grandfather clock and a secretary (desk.)"

Bob Farina, proprietor of "Over the Rainbow," a communal Montclair vegetarian shop, is troubled by the upscaling of his hometown of nearly four decades. Photo by Mia Song. Run date, March 13, 2006.

9

SOMEWHERE, 'OVER THE RAINBOW'

Montclair trend is trouble for an 'oasis'

The little vegetarian shop called "Over the Rainbow" is a rough-around-the-edges cafe sandwiched amid upscale boutiques on Montclair's trendiest strip, Church Street.

Here, owner Bob Farina has set his communal table — paper towel sheets for placemats — and offered an "All You Can Eat" crock pot buffet for $3.99, far less than even an appetizer at the many 4-star restaurants nearby.

Soon, though, it's likely to be the shop's twilight, as rising rents compel another old-line retailer to pack up, the neon "Vegetarian Foods" sign with its announcement of "Juice Bar" and "Vitamins" to shine no more.

Here, past the outdoor table of budget-priced greens and potatoes, past the "satisfactory" health placard in the window, you'll pull open a wood storm door, painted green, its wire-mesh screen clearly a homemade repair.

Inside, you'll see blankets lining a one-time cooler case, home to a Daisy's raisin bran snack here, an Utz chips bag there. And you'll find a bearded, wool-capped baritone who, when he isn't singing in a church choir, is welcoming not just the regulars but the homeless in from the rain.

"They sit down, watch some TV, buy some tea. If it gets busy, they get up, go outside," he says matter-of-factly.

There's a big dose of frugalness here, too.

It's a place of hand-penned signs on yellow poster board, with such offerings as "Burger with hummus, $3.25." The collection of dining chairs runs from a couple of thin, black high-backed ones to simple wood seats that could be hand-me-downs from a church. A small sign by the counter reads, "Chairs needed. Folding OK."

"We're not out to sell a garden salad at $7. For $7, I could get 14 heads of lettuce and feed 30 people," Farina says.

The entertainment comes in the form of VHS rentals from the library, just down the street. As dinner hour neared late Friday, all of a sudden, some eight customers lined up as the TV screen flashed a documentary on English church choirs, with a heavy dose of organ music and hymn-singing.

"It sounds like church," said one of the arrivals, Dottie Mock.

And in some ways, it is.

Susan Newton stops to say Farina was particularly attentive when she had to restrict her diet during pregnancy, making her an "awesome" dessert. "He's like my brother, and he works with you on prices," she said. "I don't know what I would do without him . . . and I mean that from my heart."

Soon, Gypsy Rain walks in. Typically, she said, she has special-needs adults in tow, from the ARC. "Eight course meals for $5," she said of the allure. "It's an oasis. . . . It's our special place. . . . I do not want them to close."

Judgment Day is not as close as the shop's movie poster of Cecil B.DeMille's "The Ten Commandments" suggests, with actor Charlton Heston as Moses, arms raised far above his head, about to cast down the weighty tablets carrying God's rules to live by.

The shop's lease, Farina said, runs out in several months, a situation likely to push up his monthly rent of $1,740 by several hundred dollars. Seeing the day coming, he was going to sell the business, first situated across the street and in this locale for eight years, for a few thousand, but it fell through, he said.

At a slower moment, he sits in his arm chair as a customer hands him two quarters. "What's that Mel?" he asks. He's shown a Granny Smith apple. "I owe you a nickel."

From Farina's perspective — father of three, grandfather of two — the upscaling of his hometown of nearly four decades is troublesome. He's seen the bronze horse at a nearby antique store, priced at tens of thousands of dollars, he said.

"There's so many people in need, what's the purpose of that?" he says.

Andy Luria, who has worked alongside Farina all eight years at this location, has seen the working class shops, such as the nurses' uniform store, move on.

But he knows something of business cycles, the kind that historically keep introducing economic downturns at the most inopportune times.

"Then it will be working folks coming back again," Luria says.

Former Montclair Mayor Grant M. Gille says the township had high hopes for this building when it was purchased in 1980 to be the new town hall. Photo by John Munson, Run date, May 22, 2005.

10

FUNCTION OVER BEAUTY

In Montclair, town hall gets little respect

On one wall is an artist's romanticized rendering of Montclair's main library. Nearby is a framed knit throw depicting scenes of Montclair High School's outdoor amphitheater, the neoclassical art museum, the imposing lines of the historic Lackawanna train station.

What's missing among these public treasures - displayed inside Montclair's council chambers - is any depiction of, well, town hall.

The seat of government - basically a square box, a retrofitted office building - turns 25 this month, and to paraphrase Rodney Dangerfield, it doesn't get much respect. The kindest remark heard there one recent morning was that it's "functional."

"It looks a lot older than 25," Mayor Ed Remsen said.

Katya Wowk, the town's webmaster, said it can withstand the elements, some of them anyway. "It keeps the wind out. We didn't say anything about the rain."

Gerald Tobin, who is leading a new facilities advisory committee that will be putting the place under a microscope, was blunt.

"It just doesn't present the greatest image for the town," said Tobin, a councilman. "It's undistinguished architecturally, to say the least, and basically it doesn't project anything you'd want to project in a town like Montclair."

It was on May 30, 1980, when Montclair Mayor Grant M. Gille signed on the dotted line, closing on the $1.75 million purchase of 205 Claremont Ave. and allowing the move from the circa 1913 municipal building at Valley Road and Bloomfield Avenue and the consolidation of other satellite offices.

"This would be a wonderful town hall," said Gille of the thinking back when the town discussed buying the 1970 office building being vacated by computer company Sperry Univac. "It had parking, which we never had. And an elevator."

But like the shine on a showroom-fresh automobile, appreciation has dimmed.

At the tail end of his term in 2000, then-Mayor William Farlie went for the escape hatch, looking to consolidate functions further by merging the administrative offices of the school system and the town into the vacant Montclair Community Hospital.

"That was like the perfect storm, the perfect time for those two things to come together," he said.

They didn't. He, too, says Montclair's seat of government leaves much to be desired.

"Besides physically being problematic, the present town hall doesn't overwhelm you with a sense that this is really a progressive, bright, sharp kind of operation."

If only it was like Little Falls' new and imposing town hall in a classical style.

"I did see that," Tobin said. "I said, 'Wow, oooh, look at that.'"

Farlie, too, sounded impressed.

"Can you believe that?" Farlie asked. "It looks like the halls of Congress, practically. We'd have a hard time doing something so grandiose. I'm just stunned every time I go by it, that they had the nerve to build something like that."

Little Falls Mayor Eugene Kulick said no nerve was needed.

"How can it be extravagant if we paid $2.3 million for it?" Kulick asked. "People build houses for that."

Erected in 2001 on township-owned land, the town hall is topped with a windowed copula with a weather vane depicting a bird in flight. Inside the wood doors, the two-story circular atrium features a wide center staircase rising to a landing with large historical pictures from the town's past. There's even a large potted tree.

Architects have come calling for a look-see, Kulick said. "They were shocked" at what they saw, he said. "Some of these guys are telling me, 'You can't build a building for less than $4 million.'"

But build it they did. John Bleeker of the Haledon-based Bleeker Architectural Group was at the design controls.

Asked whether the style would be fitting for Montclair, he said: "You want something that has a small-town feel to it. I would think that something that has a similar feel as the Little Falls building would probably be most appropriate. The building should not be a converted office building."

Montclair's town hall is made of whitish brick, punctuated by rows of brown aluminum windows. Inside the front doors is a bright orange directory, fastened to dark paneling. One wall, by the elevator, has blotches of plaster protruding from the wall surface, what's left after a marble sheet was removed months ago.

"Now, it's modern art," Tobin joked.

Talk of building a new town hall turns to discussion of hurdles.

Less than a year ago, Montclair dedicated a new $4.8 million fire headquarters. Still ahead is the start of a new $35 million elementary school. What's more, Township Manager Joseph Hartnett, in his annual budget message, raised red flags about the long-term impact of the town's debt.

"I'd love to have a new town hall. I just haven't figured out how to do it yet," Tobin said. "It may be, unfortunately, beyond our means, unless we come up with some creative way to do it."

"I think it will be opportunistic," Farlie said.

When the borough of West Long Branch went looking for a new town hall, they found one in an old church, the Calvary Assembly of God.

"It still looks like a church. . . . We took the steeple off. Now we have a clock tower there," said Lori Cole, the borough clerk.

There, as in most places, the idea was cost-saving consolidation of government services. In Montclair's case, there are 67 staffers at town hall, and at its school board offices on Valley Road, 38 employees.

Back in Gille's term, he said, he was of the mind to acquire the corner house next to the new town hall for expansion. That didn't happen. Remsen said the current location is workable with, perhaps, a partnership with the board of education.

"Right now, I don't see it on our short list," however, he said.

Today, Gille's name is forever etched on a brass plaque reading "Montclair Town Hall." It is dated May 30, 1980.

"There are prettier town halls," Gille said, but "I think it's served the town pretty well for a quarter of a century."

The municipality of Montclair has adopted a "Fair-Trade" resolution for the local government, reflecting a movement as advertised at the Terra Tea Salon & Fair Trade Eco Market. Photo by Jerry McCrea. Run date, Nov. 4, 2008.

11

MONTCLAIR BREWS FAIR-TRADE JAVA
Tries to blend commerce, economic justice

Maxwell House Special Delivery has been the java of choice in Montclair's town hall, where a coffee machine in a hallway off the manager's office provides the daily caffeine fix.

But Maxwell House's "good to the last drop" blend, which traces its aromatic origins to 1892 and whose slogan is attributed to a 1907 comment by President Theodore Roosevelt, might not be welcome there anymore.

In its place might be the fair-trade variety — the product of a resolution, adopted by the governing body, that declares Montclair to be a "fair-trade town."

Look for the fair-trade label on the java being sipped by Montclair's elected councilors at conference meetings, by staffers at the libraries, perhaps even on town-purchased cotton Little League uniforms, all in the name of economic justice and environmental sustainability.

"It's a means to an end. None of these items come with big price tags . . . really just a few cents more," Mayor Jerry Fried said after last month's unanimous vote making Montclair the first in New Jersey to wave the "fair-trade" banner.

For one, Stephanie Sheerin is thrilled with the resolution, which establishes "a policy to maximize the purchase of fair-trade certified coffee, tea, sugar and other products in the process of procuring necessary goods" for Montclair's government.

She's the one who approached Fried after stirring the fair-trade pot at Montclair's First Congregational Church with a "It's Only Fair" holiday sale, something that mushroomed into fair trade teas, fashion shows and, of course, the post-worship rite of coffee hour.

For her, the seeds were planted some 17 years ago, she said, when the new Rutgers-New Brunswick grad volunteered for an 18-month stint in Kenya. "I saw firsthand the difference it could make in someone's life when they had decent employment," she said.

Perhaps nowhere is the fair-trade fervor more prevalent than at Terra Fair Trade Eco Market and Tea Salon on Montclair's Church Street.

Outside, the window is filled with fair-trade notices, from one touting the governing body's declaration to another advocating the pre-Halloween sale of certified chocolate under the heading "Fair Trade is Boo-Tiful."

Inside, java drinkers sit at small tables as they sip fair-trade certified drinks. The shelves are lined with Equal Exchange coffee beans, priced $10.25 a bag, and a Green Mountain fair trade blend from the Kenyan Highland Cooperative, for $9.75.

The gift merchandise is crafted from raw materials readily available in developing countries: rice bags from Vietnam turned into shopping bags, a tote bag made from juice cartons in the Philippines, tin can art from South Africa, and organic cotton plush toys from South Africa.

"This is really more than a store. This is a vision," said Kate Jackson, who was manning the cash register last week. "It's really an attempt to be more than a place of commerce."

Montclair is in the vanguard of fair trade towns, whose numbers are in single-digits in the States but reach into the hundreds in the United Kingdom and Europe. (The U.S. organizer can be found at transfairusa.org)

"Montclair leads the way again," said Joseph Hartnett, the township manager. "We'll bring it up at a department head meeting, looking at our purchase practices . . . It's going to take a while to sort that out."

The criteria to get on the list includes having houses of worship that serve-fair trade products; schools that embrace fair trade, such as the Fair Trade Club at Montclair High; and stores and restaurants that offer at least two fair-trade products.

There is no shortage of those in Montclair, with The Bread Company on Walnut Street, Go Lightly on South Fullerton Avenue, Gifts at 16 on Church Street and Whole Foods on Bloomfield Avenue among the fair trade sellers who get to display the fair-trade seal in their windows.

With an economic downturn in full swing, Sheerin knows the angst about spending more for fair-trade products, which she said can be found affordably priced everywhere from Trader Joe's to Costco.

"Right now, people are really nervous, 'Oh God, the last thing I want to do is pay more,'" she said. "It can give us a chance to empathize with those having trouble making ends meet . . . (but) it really won't register on anyone's taxes."

At town hall now, the coffee varieties run from a Stop & Shop brand called Honduras San Marcos Estate in the recreation department to Folger's Classic in the clerk's office — obtained out of pocket from the municipal employees.

The designation — which comes with voluntary goals rather than obligatory ones — doesn't extend to personal purchases, but Hartnett said fair trade is taking a front seat at town hall. "We'll certainly encourage it," he said.

At Kraft, the maker of Maxwell House, meanwhile, spokesman Richard Buino said the food giant has since 2003 aligned itself with the Rainforest Alliance, which has its own sustainable farm management guidelines and its own seal, featuring the image of a frog.

"We do sell Yuban coffee in the U.S. that's Rainforest Alliance. We have eight different Rainforest products," he said. "We are the biggest buyer of Rainforest-certified coffee in the world."

Montclair homeowner Penny Weissman sits on her partially complete front porch at Columbus Avenue. Photo by Robert Sciarrino. Run date, July 7, 2004.

12

MONTCLAIR REDISCOVERS THE FRONT PORCH
Homeowners build additions in droves

There's no shortage of classic rocking-chair porches, the stuff of old Norman Rockwell prints, in suburban Montclair.

Penny Weissman, though, didn't have a sweeping open-air portal to her neighborhood — until now.

At her Columbus Avenue home, her builders, Brian Heffernan and Todd Kuipers of Quest Contracting in Sparta, were busy putting the finishing touches on it.

"They're pretty transforming," Heffernan said. "Of all the things you can do for visuals, this is it. . . . They love it, and we're not even done yet."

There has been a flurry of porch add-ons of late. Weissman's neighbor across the street, Mary Ann Cucci, is getting one too.

"We're doing it at the same time. It's funny," Cucci said. "You see the big porches on the Victorians in the Estate section. I don't see why we can't have them here."

Sometimes, rocking-chair porch wannabes simply can't, finding themselves coming up short on front-yard setbacks and the like.

"It's not easy to do, even for something that doesn't hurt your eyes," said Richard Charreun, the Montclair planning technician who fields zoning questions from porch hopefuls.

On Montclair's Marion Road, this summer's arrival of a sweeping front porch on an otherwise flat, "monolithic looking" Colonial was a long-awaited event for Dennis and Karen Casey, even if they had to give up the idea of having a gazebo-shaped corner piece.

"We were over that by a foot, so we just modified our footprint," Dennis Casey said. "There was initial disappointment, but when all was said and done, it worked out fine."

Daniel Sargeant is still waiting to hear the fate of his application to add a front porch on his Squire Hill Road home, on a block devoid of porches and where the houses visually line up.

He's originally from Panama, he said, a place rich in verandas. His wife, Yvonne, read a magazine piece a couple years ago about the comeback of the front porch, he said. Hence the decision to seek a variance from setback requirements.

"This is going to be a hurdle," Sargeant said.

It's not that Montclair's board of adjustment, which rules on variances, wants to be a spoiler. For one, its rule book says a front-porch setback has to be "in keeping" with the average front-yard setback of the three nearest principal structures.

"One of the commissioners said, 'I'm dying to put one on my house, too,'" Casey said of his public hearing.

The motivation to undertake the addition of a classic front porch can be deep-seated.

"My wife has wanted it since we moved in," Casey said. That, he said, was 20 years ago.

For Weissman, a science teacher at Montclair Kimberley Academy, her college days at the State University of New York tugged at her heartstrings.

"When I was in college, I had a porch, and I loved it. It was a very social thing. Living off campus, our street was one of the main streets, so people always had to pass by."

The same throwback to another time could be found in Cucci's explanation to add a full front porch. "We came from a farmhouse in the Hudson Valley," Cucci said.

So why did they settle for house sans sweeping porch in the first place?

"There weren't a lot of houses for sale with porches," Weissman said of the search some nine years ago. "They were few and far between." So she settled.

Now, though, she is being vigilant in her pursuit of just the right porch style. She even knocked on doors.

"I actually modeled the porch after a house on Christopher Street, with some variation," she said. "I actually went and knocked on the door and asked the woman if I could take pictures of the house, and I gave them to the architect."

Shops line Bloomfield Avenue in Montclair, where the "not wanted" list has grown to include new-car showrooms and drive-through banks. Photo by Jim Pathe. Run date, Feb. 26, 2006.

13

MONTCLAIR'S LEAST WANTED

Upscale town gives them thumbs down

They are the underbelly of an increasingly trendy business strip dubbed "The Montclair Mile."

Grandfathered in Montclair's central business district but not necessarily loved, auto repair shops, tattoo parlors, and now new-auto dealerships and rent-a-car outfits share space on a blacklist, the so-called "prohibited use" lineup.

Places with such names as Tuptim Thai Cuisine are in; the hubcap society of Kevin McDonough's auto service center is out.

"It's a shame, but I guess that's where they want this town to go: restaurants," McDonough said. "To me, it certainly seems like they're trying to make this another Hoboken."

In the past decade, Montclair's "not wanted" list has grown from such operations as used-car dealers, check-cashing outfits, pawn shops and adult entertainment to this month's newest add-ons: new-car showrooms, such as Montclair Jaguar; drive-through banks, such as the newest and apparently final one at Commerce Bank; and rental-car outfits, of which there are none.

For those in place, being "grandfathered" means they can keep operating but have little hope of expanding or selling to an expansion-minded buyer. That rubs Ed "Ox" Occhipinti the wrong way.

"The town handcuffs you," he said of his one-time intention of expanding Jinx Proof Tattoo & Body Piercing.

"You can't get to your American Dream. . . . It's disgusting, actually," he said of the prohibitions. "It actually just makes me very angry."

Besides, he said, his business is misunderstood. The clientele is not just bikers anymore, he said. "It's doctors, lawyers. . . . Mothers with their daughters come to get their bellybuttons pierced. The demographics have really changed."

Keeping out businesses perceived as undesirable is nothing new.

Deborah Kole of the New Jersey League of Municipalities said business-district prohibitions include everything from abortion clinics, fortune tellers and discos in Caldwell to discount stores, auction houses and coin-operated laundries in Franklin Lakes.

"The answer is, there's a variety of things that are prohibited," she said.

Just last year, Maplewood effectively barred nail salons in the upscale Maplewood Village by setting a distance limit between shops and extended the prohibition to nail and hair salons along a "pedestrian retail zone" on Springfield Avenue.

The roadblocks were well-received by the salons, said Vic De Luca, a committeeman and former mayor. "They wanted their clients to come in and do other types of shopping," he said.

Tom Lonergan, who as executive director of the Montclair Center Business Improvement District is spearheading the struggle for the "right mix" along the Montclair Mile, acknowledged the abundance of nail salons there but wouldn't say whether they might ever show up on Montclair's prohibited list.

"Let's just say the BID is always looking at ways to improve the diversity of our retailers," he said.

From McDonough's perspective — a makeshift sign in his shop reads "94th anniversary" — the Montclair Mile's abundance of restaurants is a problem in itself. "If you wanted to buy a suit in this town, there's no retail. . . . In time, they (new arrivals) will demand a retail presence in town. It's going to be an interesting five to 10 years."

Sometimes, a business can come perilously close to a prohibited use. That's what happened when Montclair Video in 2003 displayed such items in its window as "The Erogenous Zone" game and "LoveJam" lotion.

More recently, red flags went up over window displays at Dressing for Pleasure Exotic Lingerie.

"They came into compliance," Lonergan said of the run-ins.

Back on the auto side, Allen Swett, the sales manager at KOS MotorCars, defended his turf. "They can't overlook the fact a lot of these businesses have been around a long while and serve a purpose," he said.

In minutes, Walter Kos, the owner, emerges from the back room and talks with fondness of his collection of old classic cars, many ripe for restoration. There's a 1951 Bentley, a "collector's car" that's been lying in wait for 18 years, he said.

"It's gorgeous, all the woodwork," he said. "It went from England to South Africa and then to here. . . . They all need a little work."

The showroom window today presents just two cars to passers-by, one of them a rare red 1968 BMW 1600, he said. Soon, they hope to open up the wall with windows and display more of the collection. It's not an expansion, though.

"We're doing whatever we can to add value — in the (building's) footprint," Swett said.

Tom Moloughney, owner of Nauna's Bella Casa in Montclair, and head chef Ricky Doyle present examples of the cuisine they offer at the restaurant. Photo by Jim Pathe. Run date, March 12, 2006.

14

PASTA AND SAUCE, PLEASE, AND HOLD THE CORNED BEEF

Sons of Erin offer Italian food in Montclair

Tom Moloughney's ancestors hail from County Tipperary in Ireland. His head chef has the Irish-sounding name of Ricky Doyle. The first manager you're likely to see is Sean Gleeson, whose lineage extends to Galway.

Yet, this place is Nauna's Bella Casa, home of the new Piazza dining room in Montclair, a destination where visitors emerging from their cars might hear the piped-in, soothing voice of Italian tenor Andrea Bocelli singing "Tu Ci Sei," translation "You Are There."

You'd be somewhere, all right, but where? All those Irish surnames. All those Italian dishes.

"Don't make fun of an Irish guy running an Italian restaurant," said Moloughney, whose ancestors were stubborn enough to resist the Americanization of the name to Maloney. "My great-great grandfather said, 'No, we're not changing our name.'"

But change they did. A Moloughney married a Dalesandro. A Doyle wed a Cuarino. And elsewhere, the great melting pot did its handiwork, with the American theater noticing and then staging such shows as "Joey & Mary's Irish-Italian Wedding."

Irish-Italian ties, in fact, run deep. James Joyce, the celebrated writer, wrote "Dubliners" while in Trieste, Italy. The Irish have been called the "Sicilians of the North." An Irish monk by the name of Cathal, for Charles, became Saint Cataldo, whose name is attached to towns and churches all over the Italian peninsula.

Dermot Quinn, an expert on Irish-American culture at Seton Hall University and author of "The Irish in New Jersey: Four Centuries of American Life," recalls a Boston legislator whose district was half-Irish, half-Italian.

"He use to joke it was a combination of Gaelic and garlic," he said.

As for Moloughney, he came on to run Nauna's (Italian, for grandma's) in Montclair back in the 1980s, partnering with two "full-blooded" Italians, he said. After all, the guy who founded Domino's Pizza has a name with a particularly Irish ring to it, namely Tom Monaghan.

It was a small takeout place, he said, teetering between making money and losing money. Then things changed. "Ever since then, they joke it took an Irishman to come in and make everything profitable," Moloughney said.

It wasn't until some 18 months ago that he brought in Doyle as head executive chef, who coincidentally had run an Italian restaurant of his own, named Toscani in Belleville. There, he said, he went by the name "Ricky Dee."

"Ricky Doyle as an Italian chef didn't seem right," he said.

Over the years, his Italian genes became more firmly ingrained. "I married an Italian girl, too. My wife's 100 percent Italian." Together, they had a son, now a 19-year-old college freshman. His name: Mario Doyle. "Kids tease him at school."

Moloughney, too, has had to adapt.

"Every time I talk to a salesman, an insurance broker . . . they ask your name. . . . 'Tom Moloughney,'" he says. "You hear a chuckle, 'You sure you own this place?' I've heard it hundreds of times."

Yet, you're not likely to see him wearing a T-shirt announcing "Kiss me, I'm Irish," or even one with "Italian and proud of it."

"You know, being half and half, I never got that bravado," he said.

But a few years ago, Moloughney did embark on a trip to Ireland.

With him, he said, was Billy Tierney of the famed Irish pub, Tierney's, just a stone's throw from Nauna's. With them, too, were two friends, police officers by the name of Frank Gowen and James Marinaro, he said.

Last year at Nauna's, where the Italian decor extends to seat fabric with pictures of wine bottles labeled Dolcetto (Italian, for "little sweet one"), Moloughney and Doyle re-discovered some of their own Irish roots.

They offered up a St. Patrick's Day menu of shepherd's pie, corned beef and cabbage and the like. "We did it almost as a joke," he said. "We sold out in like 2 hours."

So this year, Doyle will be turning out the dishes of the Emerald Isle, ones he has been adept at for many years. "I guess it's in the genes," Doyle said of his Irish recipes. "The Irish genes. Can't get them out."

Out at the front counter, Gleeson — who claims to be "all Irish" — can't seem to wait.

"Oh, it's really good. The corned beef. The shepherd's pie. I love that kind of stuff." For a man who's written up a lifetime of orders for such dishes as veal Milanese and primavera, he's used to being, well, mistaken for something he's not.

"A lot of people think I'm Italian," Gleeson said. "I don't know why. Blond hair and blue eyes."

As Nauna's takes a brief respite from the all-Italian menu, though, other entrepreneurs are just getting started.

Across the street, a couple doors from Romano's Deli, a sign announces the arrival of a new business. "Coming Soon! Joe Bartoni's Italian Market. Now Hiring," it reads.

Jim Francoise, who owns The Olympic Shop in Montclair with his mother and siblings, and employee Dorothy Carey prepare merchandise for the store's going-out-of-business sale. The shop was started by Francoise's father in 1945. Photo by Jim Pathe. Run date, Oct. 19, 2006.

15

THE LAST LAP FOR A CHAMPION

Since 1945, retailer cared for clients, staff

In 1957, a barely 10-year-old boy named Jim Franciose darted across the street with his $2-a-day earnings from his father's store, The Olympic Shop.

"I went across the street to Burrey's music center and bought two 45s," he said. "Ricky Nelson's 'Be Bop Baby,' and 'Alone,' by The Shepherd Sisters. I still have them."

The record shop closed long ago. But The Olympic Shop - founded just after World War II by his world-class bicyclist father, Mickey - hung on. So did Jim.

There, his customers encountered row upon row of those dressy button-down pinpoint Oxfords and preppie neckties with that collegian flair. The well-tailored salespeople knew all the wrinkles in how to dress a blue-chip clientele.

But now, The Olympic Shop, the oh-so-proper clothier that has been a fixture in Upper Montclair Village since November 1945, is in its final throes. And Jim Franciose, now 59, is in the midst of saying farewell after a "heart-wrenching" decision to close the landmark.

"We try to keep it family-oriented," he said of his 14 staffers as the 13,000-square-foot clothier readied for today's start to a weeks' long "quitting business" sale. "The people were known as the Olympic family, and the family's splitting up."

It was part economics.

"The family decided that this real estate was worth more as a rental property than a retail store," he said.

And part the lack of anyone to take up the torch.

"It's always nice to pass something off to your children," he said. "Neither of my children were interested, and the rest of my family lives down in North Carolina, so that cuts down on the options."

Standing side by side with Franciose these next few weeks is Steve Mazur, a Denver-based retail consultant who has run "end of an era" sales coast to coast since 1984.

"They use to call me Mr. New Jersey," he said. He has closed them all, he said. "From Plainfield, to Asbury Park, to Little Silver."

Now he was in Montclair, running the going-out-of-business promotion and doing some hand-holding. "What they don't know yet," he said of the Olympic Shop staff, "is the funny feeling when all that's left are the little dust bunnies."

Lynn Ciallella is already is the midst of separation anxiety.

"Incredibly sad. Incredibly sad," she said as she and co-worker Kirat Walia undertook the tedious task of repricing lingerie on the shop's second floor.

In a "lifetime" of reporting to The Olympic Shop, she has dressed generations of families and become part of another. "I met my husband here," she said of her early days in the 1970s. "I danced with Jim's dad at my wedding."

It was Jim Franciose's late father, Nicholas "Mickey" Franciose, who started the shop after the war interrupted his path to hoped-for glory in the 1940 Olympics. In the battle of Anzio, Italy, the elder Franciose suffered leg wounds that resulted in nine operations.

"He was three-time national amateur champion. He would have had a good chance," Jim Franciose said of his father's cycling career.

His trophy from a victory in the 1939 Melbourne Grand Prix - as well as the Carbine racing bike he pedaled that day - are mounted in the store's two-story entryway. So too is the head of a moose, something that gave the clothier a manly feel.

"A lot of little kids come by the sidewalk just to see the moose. 'Look at the moose!' On Christmas, we'd put a Santa hat on it," said Franciose, whose smile speaks volumes of the warm memory.

There are others. By the back entrance is a stained-glass window of four racing cyclists, a birthday gift from Jim, the son, to his father, in 1986. Look closely, and the gift, set in a much larger picture window, is attached with a wide silver-colored tape.

"That's been up there 20 years, a testimonial to duct tape," said Franciose, breaking a slight smile.

Nowhere is the shop's persona more evident than in Franciose, who sports a navy blue blazer, gray trousers and piercing blue eyes.

There is a certain reserve to this man who studied English literature at the private Hamilton College and went on to get his juris doctor degree at Syracuse University. For a while, he even clerked for a judge in Sussex County. But he has no regrets about forgoing a career in law for a one in retail not quite as rosy as his father first suggested back in the mid-1970s.

"No. No. There's too many attorneys out there," he said of the competition.

Evidence of his academic background - and his retailing savvy - can be found in the shop's framed quotation attributed to John Ruskin, the 19th century English essayist.

"There is hardly anything in the world that some man cannot make a little worse and sell a little cheaper," it reads, "and the people who consider price only are this man's lawful prey."

Dick Davies - who knew Franciose as a frat brother at Hamilton's Chi Psi fraternity - knows all about that.

He stepped into Franciose's shop in 1975, he said, about to make the leap from the construction trades to the professional world.

Those blue suits. "They wore like iron," Davies said. Those heavy horsehide shoes, the Cordovan Imperial wingtips. "They'll last forever," Davies said. "Per-day, they cost nothing."

The care extended to advice on the proper dress-shirt collar, whether a Windsor or a button-down, he said, something he recalls Jim Franciose helping him with personally. "It was adding to your knowledge, to give you confidence to go anywhere," Davies said.

The one-time frat brother became president of a couple of companies, a consultant to Fortune 500 companies and even taught corporate dress at universities. "I don't know if he knows his effect on my life, but it's huge," he said.

Photographer Phil Cantor prepares to take a group portrait of the Montclair Police Department in front of headquarters. It was the first group shot of the department in more than 50 years. Photo by Joe Epstein. Run date, May 8, 2007.

16

OFFICERS PUT ON A BIG SMILE FOR SHOT IN HISTORY BOOKS

Portrait records 50 years worth of service

David Sabagh has one of those old-fashioned photographs of the Montclair police force hanging in his police chief's office. It's dated 1926. The latest — from 1946 — hangs nearby.

It seems those old-style panoramic portraits — showing poker-faced officers in blue standing shoulder to shoulder — fell out of style.

Until yesterday.

His uniformed force — nearly all 111 save for a few absences — hit the elevated stage and rows of fold-out metal seats outside headquarters yesterday to capture their image for posterity. They slipped on white gloves. They adjusted their dress-hat visors. Some even smiled.

"We only do this once every 50 years," Sabagh said.

Peter Miscia, a patrolman who serves as the commander of Montclair's nascent honor guard, was the afternoon's master of ceremonies for a noticeably more diverse police force.

"Fall in. Fall in," Miscia yelled as the 3 p.m. event unfolded outside the circa 1913 corner headquarters.

"Don't argue with him. He's got a gun," one of the unarmed officers softly shot back.

Miscia, who as part of the honor guard also had a sword hanging from his belt, was looking forward to the end of this assignment.

"It's like trying to organize a bunch of grumpy mice," he said.

Photographer Phil Cantor, who otherwise snaps pictures of beaming white-gowned ladies tossing bouquets, approached Sabagh with the idea of a group portrait. Cantor said he has a fondness for those old shots of doughboys in their military grab.

"I was always fascinated by those giant battalion photos from World War I," said Cantor, who runs a photography studio on busy Bloomfield Avenue.

A few passers-by stopped and gawked. "The troops," one woman said as she walked by with an arm-full of library books.

The main lens was a Fuji 6x17 Panorama, a loaner from the camera-maker that retails, he said, for $5,000. "This is the monster," he said.

This shoot had logistical challenges all its own.

"See how the ground slopes? We're putting all the tall guys on that end," Cantor said while pointing to the lower side of Valley Road. "Just to even it out."

It was a quite a change of pace for Cantor, fresh from a weekend shoot taking individual shots of children on a T-ball team.

"I'm going to give you a 1, 2, 3 — fire," Cantor yelled out to the supervisors and officers.

A voice emerged from the ranks. "Oh, don't say that."

Before the first shutter even clicked, Cantor sat on a metal folding chair in front of the ranks giving instructions.

"Don't sit so far back in your chairs. Come slightly forward. One leg forward," he said.

Unlike the portraits of old, this one shows off the equipment: three Harley-Davidson Road Kings and a showroom-fresh 2007 Dodge Charger that idles using only four of its six cylinders for fuel efficiency. Not that Sabagh doesn't appreciate the vintage variety.

"They had station wagons, stick-shifts, which was great," Sabagh said of his counterparts a half-century ago. "They had character."

As for the motorcycle cops, they still had a vintage look. They packed their gun belts and lifted their left legs atop the yellow painted curb, giving a good view of their black knee-high boots.

It was something of a power trip for Cantor, positioned with his three tripod-held cameras atop an 8-by-8 platform surrounded by yellow tape reading "POLICE LINE. DO NOT CROSS."

In a post-shoot gathering, the old 1946 photograph sparked a quick ancestry-like hunt to identify the chief in the picture. Everyone could point him out. But naming him was another matter.

"The older records. Every chief filed things differently," Sabagh said of the lack of information as he searched some files.

Soon, Deputy Chief Roger Terry, the department's most senior member with 34 years on duty, rang up former Police Chief Edward Giblin, who retired long ago. The unidentified chief from 1946, it turns out, was Tim Fleming, he said.

As officers left with their dress blues on hangers after the voluntary call-up, Sabagh checked up on any crime stats during an hour when coverage was provided by police from Verona, Glen Ridge, the Essex County Sheriff's Department and Montclair State University.

An initial report is that a visiting officer had to shoot an injured deer felled by a vehicle.

"It figures. We have coverage for one hour, and a gun is discharged," he said. But in seconds, he learns that wasn't the case. No gun was fired. The deer was DOA.

That left only one other notable police response, apparently.

"A juvenile throwing rocks at a school bus," he said.

Restaurant owner Bobby Restaino clears tables. He and his wife, Connie, right, will close the doors of the Soda Pop Shop. Photos by Saed Hindash. Run date, Feb. 4, 2007.

17

BYE-BYE LOVE, HELLO NORMAL STUFF

A tasty era comes to an end in Montclair

Those aching arms reaching into the freezer for another "Gilligan's Island" pop parfait.

Those heavy platter-filled serving trays with an "Aunt B.L.T, Mayberry's favorite sandwich" on one end, an "Arnold the Pig Burger, Straight from Mr. Ziffle's pen" on the other.

An apron-wearing Connie Restaino has been working the tables at the retro Soda Pop Shop in Montclair for the better part of her 10-year-old son Cameron's life. Now, she's longing wistfully for a simpler "Ozzie & Harriet" kind of life.

"Down time and family, that's it. Getting dinner on the table, normal everyday stuff that people take for granted," she said a few days ago as she sat down in a booth of hot pink and green upholstery and broke the news to her young staff.

The Soda Pop Shop — a place that drips nostalgia on Montclair's main drag — is in its final episodes. "It's been a great run," she said.

By her side for eight years now has been the show's creator, her husband, Bobby, whose "addiction" to the pop culture of the 1960s gave birth to the long-running Soda Pop Shop in 1999.

Inside the eatery's windows are the throwbacks of another era: little six-packs of red and green tree-lighting bulbs from Woolworth's, "America's Christmas Store"; six-packs of Wink, the Canada Dry soft drink marketed in the 1960s as "The Sassy One"; an array of black-and-white 8-by-10s from TV's "The Munsters" and "Lassie," to name just a few.

In fact, Jon Provost, the one-time child actor who played Timmy to TV's famous collie once showed up at the Soda Pop Shop for an evening of autograph signing, joined by other such television icons as Jay North, who played "Dennis the Menace."

The piped in music — via satellite radio — fills the room with the words of Herman's Hermits last Top 10 song, recorded in 1967: "There's a kind of hush, all over the world tonight."

Ageless, Bobby Restaino says. It has even rubbed off on Alia Baye, who at 21 has four-plus years' experience at the Soda Pop Shop and is one of the longest-running waitresses. "I go home and download it."

Late Thursday afternoon, seven waitresses and counter help quietly awaited the dinner rush. It was the day Bobby and Connie were breaking the news of the pending closing as early as Saturday to their second family.

"Why's Christine crying?" the Restaino's son, Cameron, asks his Dad.

"Because she's sad," Restaino says.

He had already shared some wisdom of his 46 years with the young staff.

"Life is like a series of doors that open and close," he said of explaining the decision to close a successful business and begin anew. "Another one will open. When they close in your life, of course it's going to be sad. That's what life is all about."

He knows that firsthand. Restaino was once a Newark firefighter who was struck by a falling object that fell from a third-story window, leaving him with back trouble and the resulting numbness, he says. Now, he's thinking of perhaps doing voice-overs for cartoons, or maybe standup comedy, or even opening an antique shop.

"Something simple where I can lock the door at 5 p.m.," he said.

And in a few years, maybe more, he might blow the dust off the retro collectibles and put the Soda Pop Shop into perhaps more profitable reruns with even more bells and whistles. The "theme" will live on, he insists.

At a corner booth, a life-size image of TV's Ed Sullivan and a smaller one of teen idol Frankie Avalon peer over his shoulder. In many ways, Restaino is an oracle of television-past.

At home in Cedar Grove, he sits himself down in front of his DVD-powered television and watches old episodes of "F Troop," a '60s sitcom about misfits stationed at "Fort Courage" in the Old West. He's even appreciates "My Mother The Car," a not-so-well-received sitcom starring Jerry Van Dyke as a guy who buys a classic 1928 Porter automobile possessed by his late mother.

"That's when TV stretched the imagination," he said. "Sometimes I just want to transport myself into the screen. I was born too late."

To be sure, Restaino has stretched the patience of some in Montclair, where he's been a vocal critic of what he calls "aggressive" ticketing by meter maids in a community he deems "unfriendly" to businesses such as his.

Montclair's downtown, now dubbed "The Montclair Mile" with arguably one of the heaviest concentrations of restaurants in New Jersey, has been going upscale amid the influx of New Yorkers.

"Very corporate. It's losing its charm," he said of the strip. "There's something wrong in Gotham as they say," he said, invoking the name of the mythical metropolis of Batman.

Tom Lonergan, the executive director of the Montclair Center Business Improvement District, said it was "crushing" to lose another iconic business.

"The loss demonstrates the challenges we're facing as a changing community," Lonergan said.

Empty storefronts have popped up right around the Soda Pop Shop as landlords have increased rents.

"It has crept up," Lonergan said of the vacancy rate. "We've gone from slightly under 5 percent to just about 7 percent in the last two months. While we respect market forces, we just question whether or not some of these rental rates are matching what the market can bear right now."

In Restaino's case, he said, it's not rising rents as much as his own reasonably priced lease, which turned out to be something of a hot commodity. "It's more lucrative to sell the lease then sell the business myself," he said.

So, for now, it's more of a season finale.

"Not happy. Not happy," Julia Gorton of Glen Ridge said while seated at a booth with her sons, Russell and Raleigh Kirk. Soon, a grilled cheese sandwich and cheese fries arrives for the self-described vegetarians.

"Montclair lacks a good family sit-down experience," she said, "a restaurant we could eat at for under $50."

Kirsten Lagatree's estate on North Mountain Avenue in Montclair might have hosted John Lennon and Yoko Ono in the 1970s. Photo by Marko Georgiev. Run date, Jan. 9, 2005.

18

FOR SALE: 5BR, 3.5BTHS, FAMOUS OCCUPANT

John and Yoko slept here.

So thinks Kirsten Lagatree, who has just found a buyer for her estate on Montclair's North Mountain Avenue, a place once home to 1970s producer/recording engineer Roy Cicala, who worked on late Beatle John Lennon's "Imagine" and "Double Fantasy" albums.

"John and Yoko came out to record. There were soundproof rooms. Whether they actually recorded there, I don't know," said Mary Tetzloff, an agent with Montclair Realty, which handled the listing.

Lagatree's house is one of several that have had famous occupants - or visitors - that find themselves on the market from time to time.

The home of a descendant of John Quincy Adams - the sixth president of the United States - on Montclair's Llewellyn Road recently was listed for $1.3 million.

"Sold" signs have gone up at the homes of actor Eddie Bracken, suffragette Lucy Stone and composer/lyricist Herman Hupfeld.

The famous pedigrees, believed to stir some interest in a listing, don't typically contribute to a sale, though, some agents say.

"I don't think the famous name inside has much value," said Carol Rhodes of Rhodes, Van Note in Upper Montclair.

Still, the "famous name" does add something to the provenance.

"I think there's a cache, that people like that connection, to be able to say, 'Look who lived here,'" said Linda Grotenstein of Coldwell Banker's Upper Montclair office.

That's just what Doris Buzvy did in the 37 years she lived at the one-time Montclair home of Lucy Stone, whose pro-suffrage views were said to have converted Susan B. Anthony to the cause.

"I heard they used to have meetings of the women's suffrage movement," she said of the Valley Road home in the English Gothic-style that she sold a few years ago. As a gift to the buyers, she left behind some books on the suffragette.

Marjorie Fierst, who lives in lyricist Herman Hupfeld's old haunt, said she received as a housewarming gift sheet music of Hupfeld's "As Time Goes By," popularized in the 1942 film "Casablanca" starring Humphrey Bogart and Ingrid Bergman.

"It was part of the charm," said Fierst, noting they had a house sale shortly after moving in. "Everybody in the neighborhood came over and told us their favorite stories."

"I always joked, 'You can feel Mae West dancing around the living room,'" said her husband, Gerald Fierst, who noted that crooner Bing Crosby and actress Mae West were Hupfeld's friends.

The Hupfeld house, too, appears to be just the right fit.

"We're all actors," he said. His son, whose family lives on the home's lower level, is a playwright and his daughter-in-law works on Broadway, he said. "There was really a feeling of a karmic connection," he said.

Sometimes, when a "For Sale" sign goes up, mum is the word. That was the case when Olympia Dukakis, who won a Oscar for 1987's "Moonstruck," put her Upper Mountain Avenue home up for sale in Montclair a few years ago.

"We were extremely discreet about showing it," Gloria Falzaer, the real-estate agent who handled the listing, said of trying to keep the simply curious at bay. The house eventually sold to some soap-opera performers, she said.

For Lagatee, the trail has been an interesting one since she purchased the house five years ago.

"All we knew was, 'Oh, it is said that John and Yoko spent the night here,'" she said. "The third floor of the house clearly has the remnants of a recording studio." There was cork on the ceiling and black fabric walls that once covered speakers, she said.

The home was Cicala's from 1969 to 1976, according to Montclair tax records, but Cicala was on the West Coast and unreachable, said his longtime business partner, John Hanti.

He described John Lennon, who was shot to death by Mark David Chapman in New York in 1980, as Cicala's "very good friend" but didn't know for sure whether Lennon and his wife, Yoko Ono, ever stayed there.

"I would say there's a very good possibility of that," however, Hanti said.

Perhaps the place with the biggest roster of famous connections was Montclair's Marlboro Inn. A brass plaque in the hostelry's entryway read, "History in the Making. They Were Looking for This Special Place."

The names that followed were a who's who of Hollywood and the Broadway stage: Gloria Swanson. Helen Hayes. Bette Davis. Olivia de Haviland. Ed Asner. June Lockhart. Victor Mature. Even comedian Rich Little, singer Linda Ronstadt and the Grateful Dead's Jerry Garcia stayed there.

Yet the inn is now being demolished, due to be replaced by a subdivision of homes.

The Glen Ridge house of Eddie Bracken, the star of director Preston Sturges' film classics "Hail the Conquering Hero" and "The Miracle of Morgan's Creek," was put up for sale shortly after his death, and sold for a little over $1 million in late 2003.

But not before bargain-seekers descended on an estate sale that included signed scripts and trophies that the star received from the National Broadcasters Hall of Fame and New York's Film Forum, and even a ceramic sign reading "WC," for water closet, over the powder room door.

And there are those places that aren't for sale, at least not yet. Yankee great Yogi Berra lives on Montclair's Highland Avenue. The boyhood home of astronaut Buzz Aldrin, who stepped on the moon right after Neil Armstrong in 1969, has been in the same family for decades in Montclair. The famous astronaut has even visited over the years.

Still, some stories are just that, stories.

Back in the 1970s, when Telly Savalas played the lollipop-stick chewing detective in TV's long- running "Kojak" series, the word around town was that he lived in an Upper Mountain Avenue mansion with distinctive Japanese architecture.

"The kids used to do these secret forays to see if they could see Telly Savalas," Grotenstein said. "It was like a military maneuver."

It turns out the owner was not Savalas, and he made it clear in the local press that people should stop bothering him, she said. That wasn't the end of it though.

"There was a rumor that Janet Jackson bought it," Grotenstein said of the singer who most recently made headlines because of her "wardrobe malfunction" at Super Bowl XXXVIII.

"That was totally unfounded."

This tiny house on a lot only 18 feet wide is thought to be the lowest-priced listing in Montclair. It's down to $117,500 from last summer's $175,000. "It looks like a little chalet," said real estate agent Lenore "Lee" Robinson of RE/MAX Village Square. Photo by Steve Hockstein. Run date, Jan. 27, 2009.

19

LITTLE HOUSE, BIG SAVINGS

Montclair home has mansions for neighbors

The tiny, circa-1890 frame house on the narrowest of lots — just 18 feet wide — is as modest as a single-family home can get so close to Montclair's stately Estate section, where one handsome six-bedroom colonial with "old world craftsmanship" is now listed at $1.49 million.

The mini-house with its small red deck is also less than a mile from the town's most expensive real-estate listing, the $7.75 million, 30-room mansion once home to Giants star Michael Strahan.

But this little old house on Cross Street is on the opposite end of the spectrum. It is, in fact, at just $117,500, believed to be the lowest-priced listing in town.

"I've been in business 20 years, and I've never had one that cheap. . . . It needs, hmmm, basically decor," said Lenore "Lee" Robinson, the listing agent with RE/MAX Village Square.

While it has a lot of traffic from potential buyers, it is still on the market, a sign of the real-estate slump. Its price has been slashed from its summer listing of $175,000. "I would have thought it would have sold right away," she said. "I just think people are so afraid."

Last month, just eight houses went under contract in Montclair, compared with 25 in December 2007 and 21 in the same month a year earlier, said Linda Grotenstein of Coldwell Banker's Upper Montclair office.

About 85 single-family homes are now on the market in Montclair — once a hotbed for multiple bids during the market's more heady days. The number of listings swells to about 150 when condos are counted.

Still, Adriana O'Toole, a Montclair agent who serves with the West Essex Board of Realtors, said that's about right for this time of year. And regardless, buyers, she said, are taking their time.

"They're very discerning," she said.

So discerning that the 16 single-family homes now under contract have been on the market an average of 115 days, slightly ahead of the Essex County average of 107 days.

The least-expensive house offers a red deck off the first-floor living room and a single second-floor bedroom, with sliding-glass doors. "It looks like a little chalet," Robinson said in real estate agent speak.

"The Hobbit house" is how one interested party described it, Robinson said.

There have been open houses. Prospective buyers walked through the first-floor 9-by-13 living room and the kitchen. They ascended the staircase to the sole shower-only bathroom and single bedroom. They went around back to a stockade fence-enclosed yard, just a few feet deep, to enter the full basement.

Just a week ago, RE/MAX agent Roy Castor showed the house to yet another prospective buyer. "He really liked the house. It's like the perfect size for a single person."

Little is known about the house's history. It isn't included in Montclair's otherwise exhaustive 1981 historic preservation survey, and it hardly could qualify as a carriage house once capable of holding horses and wagon. But a larger house, just a couple doors away on Cross Street, is described as a place built for "servants of wealthy landowners on nearby Union and Gates avenues."

Ceil Adkins, who remodeled her larger Cross Street home down the block, said some homeowners on the street have connections going back generations. One of her elderly neighbors, she said, told her that her grandparents once lived in what is now being called a chalet, not far from the 2.25-acre Porter Park.

"It's a very rare block. There is no other block like Cross Street. This is the only street for the servants that is right in the heart of the Porter Park area," she said. "We're surrounded by all these big beautiful mansions."

It's something Robinson can relate to. Her 1897 St. Luke's Place home, she said, once belonged to a coachman, a man who handled the bridles and such for a gentleman's or lady's transportation.

One of those nearby mansions near Cross Street was once the home of James J. Fielder, who served as New Jersey's governor after Woodrow Wilson assumed the presidency in 1913.

The little house's listing does describe the place as a "fixer-upper," something potential buyers seem to shy away from nowadays, said Roberta Baldwin, an agent at RE/MAX Village Square in Montclair. But just around the corner, on Orange Road, a 4-bedroom 1880 colonial being marketed at $650,000 "needs TLC," according to the listing.

Besides, someone might like the little "chalet" just the way it is.

"Beauty is in the eye of the beholder," Baldwin said. "A little love nest?"

Run date: Nov. 8, 2008

20

AN OBAMA TIDAL WAVE
Electorate bathes a town in blue

It might as well be called the suburban New Jersey capital of an Obama nation.

In Montclair, whose abundance of New York transplants has earned it the nickname the Upper West Side of New Jersey, Barack Obama pulled in a lopsided 84-plus percent of the vote on Election Day 2008.

The turnout for the Democratic presidential nominee, who became the first African-American president-elect, rivaled urban Newark's 92 percent, even surpassed some Newark wards, and cemented Montclair's liberal-leaning reputation like never before.

"Amazing. It's as blue as you can get for a suburban town. Incredible," said Chris Durkin, who as Essex County clerk had been crunching the numbers.

The trend can be traced to 1976, when Democrat Jimmy Carter beat Gerald Ford with 52.2 percent of the vote, and Montclair has never looked back. Richard Nixon won Montclair twice, Durkin said of the years preceding what became a tectonic shift.

Ever since, Democrats have been racking up bigger Montclair pluralities. By 1984, Walter Mondale had squeezed a few extra percentage points out of the Montclair electorate, capturing 56.4 percent of the vote. Then, it kept growing. Michael Dukakis broke the 60 percent barrier, Al Gore the 70 percent threshold, and now Obama the 80 percent hurdle.

Margot Sage-El, for one, has her finger on the pulse of Montclair's electorate as the proprietor of Watchung Booksellers, where a table just inside the front door carries such titles as "Dreams from My Father" and "The Audacity of Hope" by Barack Obama, with a parody titled "Goodnight Bush" tucked in the back.

"They were just constant, huge sellers for us," Sage-El said. "Well, they said Obama did really well with the highly educated."

And the well-to-do. Of all New Jersey towns with an average income exceeding $100,000, Montclair ranked first in the state in the percent of voters casting ballots for Obama, with Maplewood, Princeton and South Orange close behind.

Montclair, too, is the birthplace of Blue Wave New Jersey, a progressive outfit whose website features supporters carrying a blue Obama sign under the campaign slogan "Yes We Can." It is also a place where the "L" word is anything but taboo.

"We are unabashedly liberal," said Jerry Fried, the bike-riding Montclair mayor whose Unity Montclair slate dominated last May's municipal elections while waving a progressive banner. Nowadays, he is in the midst of reading "The Audacity of Hope," he said.

By at least one measure, Montclair is New Jersey's most liberal town. So says e-Podunk, a New York-based demographic numbers-cruncher that analyzed political contributions and election results to come up with its rankings of the "Most Liberal Places in America."

Of course, looks can be deceiving. Less than 48 hours after the polls closed, John Hickey and his wife, Jas, were seated by the Sunrise Bagels Cafe in Montclair's Watchung Plaza.

He was wearing a "Spirit of Nashville" shirt, a souvenir from his Shakle nutritional supplements convention rather than any sign of allegiance to Tennessee, where the presidential results were split, 57-42, just like New Jersey's, only Republican John McCain was the winner.

"A country shirt. Right. Amazing," said Hickey, who actually counts himself among the Montclair Obama wave.

Like so many others, the Hickeys arrived from New York, in their case the Flatbush section of Brooklyn. They came for the schools and real-estate values, at least compared with Brooklyn's Park Slope, he said.

"We never took a poll," he said of Montclair's political leaning. "We basically drew a circle around Manhattan."

The Obama story is almost identical in Maplewood, where 83.01 percent of the voters were in the "Yes We Can" camp — just 1.05 percent less than Montclair's.

"It is so overlooked. It's so blue, Maplewood. It has the same type of feel as Montclair," Durkin said.

In the quaint shopping square called Maplewood Village, native Mary Vayas went so far as to parade her political feelings in the window of her clothing and accessory shop, called No. 165.

A large color photo of Obama introducing his daughter, Sasha, to Bruce Springsteen, peers out on Maplewood Avenue, alongside a small stack of blue Obama 2008 T-shirts. Vayas witnessed the post-Election Day procession of passing children.

"Yesterday, when kids were walking home from school, they were all saying, 'Obama. Obama,'" Vayas said.

Her sales associate, Courtney Graham, had an observation, too.

"Generally, children's opinions reflect their parents," Graham said.

Her biggest political sale item were $9.95 coffee mugs carrying little etchings of the presidents, one strictly with drawings of Republican presidents, the other strictly Democrats. The latter, however, was the biggest seller.

"We reordered the Democratic one," Vayas confessed.

Back in Montclair, the degree of the Democratic tilt was not without its own set of worries.

"The only thing scary about that," Sage-El said, "is they say, 'We live in a bubble here,' and now we really do."

Even one of the Montclair GOP's own found himself in the Obama camp, nudged on by McCain's vice presidential pick, Sarah Palin.

"The Palin pick really troubled me," said Peter Zorich, a registered Republican who is a cousin of none other than the 1988 Democratic standard-bearer, Michael Dukakis. "I couldn't in good conscience vote for her. I will admit, 'Yes, I voted for Obama.'"

A line of fans waits to meet baseball Hall of Famer Yogi Berra, Photos by George McNish. Run date, June 22, 2008.

21

MY EVENING WITH YOGI

Catching their chance to meet Yankee great

They're die-hard fans of one of baseball's giants, Yankees great Yogi Berra.

He's 83 now. His prized autographed wares are hawked on yogiberra.com, with its full lineup of items running from a black-and-white picture of Yogi and Babe Ruth in 1947, for $125, to Yogi's No. 8 jersey, for $275.

So when — twice a year — the living legend and Montclair's own takes out his pen for the "Yogi Berra Autograph Night" at the stadium bearing his name, loyal fans camp out to get Yogi's signature for the cost of a $3.75 bleacher seat, cheaper than a gallon of gas.

"He's worth it," said Elizabeth Engelhardt, wearing a pink hand-decorated "MUNSON" shirt, for one-time catcher Thurman Munson, to show her Yankee pride.

She was one of a family of fans who arrived shortly after 9 a.m. Wednesday — some 8 hours before the gates opened for the pre-game signing ahead of a New Jersey Jackals minor-league bout.

It was enough to secure bragging rights to being the first in a line that would eventually swell to 200-plus. They came equipped. There was the Igloo drink cooler, the double-pack of Snapple ice tea, the doughnuts, the umbrellas (which came in handy for a passing shower), the electronic Uno Skip-Bo card game to pass the time.

And, of course, the playpen for Christian Engelhardt, son of Randy and Brynn. He's 9 months old and wearing a blue New York Yankees cap.

"That's what his godmother got him. Me," said Vicky Engelhardt, who as Randy's sister joined the family's Thursday morning trek from New Milford. She's wearing a Yankees shirt with a commemorative arm patch for the soon-to-be-retired "House that Ruth Built" and the dates 1923-2008.

The twice-a-year signings — the next one is Aug. 27 — are a chance for Yogi to be a booster for the New Jersey Jackals, whose Yogi Berra Stadium adjoins the Yogi Berra Museum & Learning Center on the campus of Montclair State University. The limit for the 2-hour event is billed as 300 bonafide autographs.

The latest event — under a "Grand Slam Grill" canopy on the main concourse — easily produced the biggest gathering of Yogi signed baseballs on the planet. Hands grasped an assortment of memorabilia, including large black-and-white pictures of the distracting, chatty catcher who managed the Yankees and the Mets and became a Hall of Famer.

"It was an honor to meet you Yogi, to know you all these years," said Elizabeth Engelhardt after getting an autograph on his latest book, "You Can Observe a Lot by Watching: What I've Learned About Teamwork from the Yankees and Life."

As for Yogi, his hand was steady, his signature script neat as a pinstripe. He offered up smiles to the cameras and an occasional comment, responding to a fan who asked him to write in his jersey number — the famed No. 8 — next to his autograph.

"The number's right there," said Yogi, pointing to the "8" on his jersey in the photograph.

The line stretching out of the stadium reflected a cross-section of travelers from near and far.

Jim Dunbar, a 37-year-old history teacher, left his Saratoga Springs, N.Y., home about 7 a.m. for the 3-hour drive. His wife, Amy, and mother, Joan, were busy applying sunscreen while his father, Gene, scouted out the field beyond the stadium fence.

"They came along for the ride," he said of his folks. "They'll probably go off and go shopping."

Kim Catalfamo of Belleville came early with 10-year-old son Joey, who has cerebral palsy. She said he will be taking to the field himself at

Yankee Stadium next month with the Challenger division of Little League baseball.

Her son has penned letters to baseball players, prompting them to write back. The first was from New York Mets third baseman David Wright, she said.

"Ryan Howard," chimed in Joey, adding the Philadelphia Phillies slugger to the list.

With less than 30 minutes before the 5 p.m. signing, one Clifton fan found himself at the end of the line. His name: Joe Maggio. "No `D.' That's the God honest truth," he said of a surname that often reminds people of the legendary "Yankee Clipper," Joe DiMaggio.

For the signing, the 38-year-old bought along a copy of "The History of American League Baseball" by Glenn Dickey. "I got this at the age of 11," he said.

Next to him, James Heike, a 21-year-old from Montclair, was thinking ahead about the autograph soon to land on his now plastic-encased baseball. He, like the others, said they wouldn't think of selling the prized signatures of a legend.

"Just something to have in my living room, tell my kids about him," Heike said.

As the last string of fans advanced, a late-arrival by the name of Larry Mastropolo of Old Tappan found himself as the last man on the Yogi-autograph lineup. As a kid, he said, he was a catcher, just like Yogi, so much so that his friends even called him Yogi.

Then, he whipped out his cell phone and showed a close-up of his pet English bulldog's mug. "My dog's name is Yogi," he said.

As for the Engelhardts, they weren't bothered that even the last to arrive got a coveted autograph after they camped out for the day.

"We're doing it again in August," Vicky Engelhardt said.

"We'll be first again," said her mother, Elizabeth.

Chanise Renae Stoute of Clifton holds nothing back during her rendition of "The Star-Spangled Banner." Photo by Jim Pathe. Run date, April 18, 2006.

22

OH, SAY, CAN YOU HEAR?

Tryouts for anthem are a perilous fight

It was a chance to hear those famed lyrics, over and over again.

The opening line of the national anthem — "Oh, say, can you see, by the dawn's early light" — has been an official get-to-your feet prompt at American ballfields longer than most can remember.

Yet before Opening Day, there are the auditions for those called to sing Francis Scott Key's "The Star-Spangled Banner." Prepare to be inspired. Prepare to grimace.

In this case, there are just 24 slots still open and 68 singers and musicians vying for a chance at 1 minute, 30 seconds of fame at one of this season's minor-league New Jersey Jackals games.

"If they don't know the words, boom, they're out," says Barbara Rudy, one of the snap-decision, pencil-toting judges who endured the renditions at Yogi Berra Stadium on the campus of Montclair State University.

The national anthem tryouts have the air of television's American Idol, with the contestants lined up 20 deep at times for their turn to step out on the field, turn toward home plate and belt it out in the direction of three judges in their own individual cubbyholes high above in the press box.

Some singers are carrying 8-by-10 glossies of themselves. The hopefuls ranged from pre-teens to those sporting touches of gray. Some of the tryouts' mothers, Rudy says, have e-mail addresses such as "divamommy" and "mydaughtersings."

But just as many are like Stephanie Vanderhave, a 27-year-old payroll company employee who lives in Waldwick and once sang in her high school and church choirs. "I pretty much just sing with the radio now," she says.

Yet her voice clicks. "Good 'perilous.' Good 'gallantly,'" scribbles Barbara Germann, the stopwatch-gripping judge who specifically grades pronunciation and looks for the singers to hit the coveted 1:30 delivery. Not too slow, not too fast.

"Sign her up," she writes, following up with the comment: "She's a keeper." And keep her they did. By day's end, her name appears on the list of 24 selected from the 68 tryouts, two of whom submitted recorded tapes.

The score-sheet scribbles — from nearly three hours of tryouts starting at 8:30 a.m. on Saturday — are not for the eyes of the singers.

"Out of tune," reads one.

"Changed key," says another.

"Didn't hit 'free'," says yet another.

And the particularly blunt: "Didn't like her."

Red flags can go up, too, if the anthem is overly embellished. "These people, when they goose it up," says Rudy, shaking her head and recalling an episode from TV's "The Simpsons" where a jazz singer drags out the song beyond all reason. "It's not a ballad, it's an anthem."

For the most part, the volunteer judges — all season-ticket holders — have musical backgrounds. Rudy's forte is playing flute with the Montclair Community Band. Hank Machuga's is instructing a high school choir in Elmwood Park. Germann's, however, is, well, more akin to being something of an efficiency expert.

In her day job, she says, she's dreaming up new policy wrinkles in the Prudential Insurance Co.'s product development offices. On game days, she's developed a habit of timing the singers the way others might schedule a trip to buy a hot dog. "For two years, I've been timing them unofficially," she says.

Johnnie Jones Tucker, for one, didn't hit a musical home run. She forgot her lines. Not once, but three times. "I know this song, but I just went blank," she says into the microphone after the first miscue.

Yet it wasn't a total loss for Tucker, a gospel singer from South Orange who sang for the Newark Bears in 2003. Rushing out of the press box, Rudy tells Tucker that she might be able to slip her into another slot, singing "God Bless America."

"She's got a great voice," Rudy says.

All agree the national anthem is a tough one to deliver, especially in front of an audience.

"I've never been so nervous, facing 2,000 stone-cold faces, and, of course, the song means so much to me," says Machuga, who's not just a judge but a ballfield-singing aficionado. His name — for another season — made the cut, as did 22 others who did well enough last year to be invited back — audition-free — for one of the 46 home games.

Some tryouts try to punt.

"I'm No. 17, Gabe Martinez, "and I've been really sick, so put up with me," the 18-year-old Bloomfield High student says into the microphone before giving his best post-cold and sniffles shot.

The umpires of song act quickly. He gets a "5," the top score, for his appearance and demeanor, basically his stance. Then he gets a "9" out of "10" for pitch. But something's wrong. "Good, but needs to be quicker," Rudy writes on her score sheet.

In seconds, she's motioning her arms to say "speed it up, speed it up." In the end, his name is absent from the list of the chosen. "Because there's so many trying out, the bar is high," Rudy says.

There were, however, some shoo-ins.

Taking the advice of his music students in Nutley, Dennis McPartland of New Milford showed up and played his trumpet. "This guy's in. . . . He gets a perfect score for the words, right?" Rudy jokes with her fellow judges.

After lugging his xylophone to the field, Thomas Lyons of Pequannock wins a spot with his ringing rendition of the national anthem.

"We'll definitely sell a lot of ice cream," Machuga says. "It sounds like an ice-cream truck."

Steven Plofker examines the grand stage, hidden for decades behind the multiple movie screens in the Wellmont Theater in Montclair. Photo by Marko Georgiev. Run date, May 16, 2006.

23

A GRAND STAGE REVEALED

New owner finds gem in Montclair

For more than a quarter-century, moviegoers have slipped into the red seats of the Wellmont Theater, a once grand Montclair movie palace that until a few weeks ago was showing avant-garde films.

Yet behind the multiplex's three screens is a cavernous place hidden in darkness and dripping with cobwebs, concealing the soaring ceiling and jaw-dropping stage of a grand theater that once sat upward of 2,000, but for decades remained a lost world.

That is, until yesterday.

A flashlight-toting Steven Plofker, a Montclair developer and husband of cosmetics diva Bobbi Brown, toured the bowels of the old theater, the ink barely dry on his contract to buy the Wellmont for a price purported to be just under $1 million.

"No one ever knew it was here," Plofker said as he and an assistant assessed the hidden square footage. "It could be a great restaurant, bar. . . . Who knows what it could be."

The multiplex, which seats a total of 903, would remain, Plofker said, provided he can find either a nonprofit or commercial operator.

"I'm not in the theater business and don't want to be," Plofker said. "But that's certainly the intention. . . . Whether it's a live theater, film, whatever."

The guide on the noon-time tour was Roberts Theatres' Gary E. Heckel, the longtime manager who inherited the Wellmont, Bloomfield's Lost Picture Show — now leased to 12 Miles West Theater — and the Chatham Cinema from Robert L. Roberts in 2002.

"He was my mentor, my best friend," Heckel said. "There's a lot of sentimentalism" in selling the theater, Heckel said. "It's like a second home to me."

By month's end, Plofker and his Seymour Street Associates intend to close on the sale. His investor-partner, he said, is Harlan Waksal, who once took the reins at ImClone after his brother was snarled in an insider-trading scandal that engulfed Martha Stewart.

Plofker teamed with Waksal before to purchase Montclair's Marlboro Inn, a famed hostelry demolished for a 10-home subdivision. But if anyone thinks the Wellmont might face a similar fate, think again, Plofker said.

"The building is in an historic district," Plofker said of a designation that affords the theater some protection. "If it wasn't in the district, we probably would have nominated it."

The Wellmont had barely been getting by financially, Heckel said.

The theater's niche was independent films. One of the last features was "Ballets Russes," a film tapping archival footage to tell the tale of rival dance troupes that fought the infamous "ballet battles" that consumed London society before World War II.

The $7.50 admission came with free coffee, a chance to buy an RC Cola and a "commercial free" film-going experience.

But a year ago, Heckel said, he stopped showing films in the larger, 500-seat theater in the old balcony. The heating simply cost too much, he said.

A few weeks ago, he decided to close the theater for a month, not just for "renovations" as the sign in the ticket booth declared but because of the slowness of the season. "This time of the year is really crummy," he said.

Yesterday morning, he was crouched down and making repairs to wires inside one of the Simplex 35mm projectors and the housing for its Christie Xenolite lamps. "First, it was duct tape, then it went to electrical (tape)," he said of the fixes.

Before the walk-through, Plofker had only a vague recollection of taking in a movie there. "I remember many years ago my sneaker got glued to the floor in some syrupy remnant of something," he said.

But yesterday's visit was more memorable. He stepped down into the orchestra pit. He toured what Heckel called the "Titanic," a zigzagging four-story stairwell whose rusting handrails take the visitor to each darkened deck, past heavy doors with peeling paint. Those were once the dressing rooms for the performers, Heckel said.

"Can you imagine when this first opened?" Heckel said while standing at the foot of the huge stage. "It must have been phenomenal."

The Wellmont — a combination of the original owner's name, Wellenbrink, and the town's name — opened in June 17, 1922, as a legitimate theater, but with the advent of talkies switched entirely to motion pictures in 1929.

That year, the big box-office draws were MGM's "The Broadway Melody," which was billed as the first "all talking, all singing, all dancing" film and went on to become the year's top-grossing movie. Movie-goers, too, took in "America's sweetheart," Mary Pickford, who starred in a drama of the American South titled "Coquette," her first talkie and one that captured her an Oscar for best actress.

It was another time, one that Heckel's mentor, Roberts, valued when he purchased the Wellmont in 1980. In the mid-1990s, Roberts won accolades from the Montclair Historical Society for retaining much of the original movie palace decor during a renovation.

The stately interior, with its elaborate arches, marble and gold leaf, largely remained. "When I see some of the movie palaces of yesterday, I think it's a total tragedy," Roberts once said. "There are so few left. In my plans to upgrade it into a multiplex, modern theater, I wanted to preserve that history."

In 2003, Montclair lost The Screening Zone — a 224-seat moviehouse operated by Clearview Cinemas. The next year, the 12 Miles West theater company was priced out and moved to Heckel's Lost Picture Show theater in Bloomfield when a developer purchased the Hinck Building at Montclair's "six-corners."

Still, Heckel rattled off a list of multiplex theaters nearby, including the six-screen Claridge up the street, the four-screen Bellevue Theater, and the 16 screens at Clifton Commons.

"It's too much," Heckel said. "You have to just count on your local people, and you run out of them quick."

Final touches are being applied to the Wellmont Theatre in Montclair, a 2,200-plus seat venue that is being restored to its original grandeur. Photo by George McNish. Run date, Oct. 26, 2008.

24

WELCOME BACK, WELLMONT
Box office open during rush to ready venue

Neil Feltz was sitting behind the thick glass of the new ticket windows at the Wellmont Theatre. The tape-backed brown paper on the box-office portal had just been peeled off. Then, the scheduled noon ticket-booth opening for New Jersey's newest concert venue in Montclair came and went.

By 12:16 p.m. Friday, though, Feltz was ready, sort of, for the first of about a half-dozen people who lined up outside as the clock ticked to tomorrow's premiere concert featuring Counting Crows, whose hits include "Mr. Jones" and "Accidentally in Love."

Up walked Ivonne Klink.

"Two tickets for Hanson. Balcony," she told the box office manager, who was maneuvering through a forest of new seat-picking software with an assist from three employees of ticket.com.

But Klink's words didn't quite reach Feltz's ears. The little opening to talk through was missing something. Andy Feltz, the managing partner of Montclair Entertainment LLC and Neil Feltz's brother, stood next to Klink on the sidewalk and had a ready answer.

"We'll have microphones here soon, no problem," he said.

The final 80-hour dash to tomorrow night's opening of the historic 2,200-plus seat theater was more a race of rabbits than tortoises.

Shortly before noon, John Herrmann, a deputy Montclair fire chief, stood under the marquee waiting for about 16 of his brethren to arrive for a get-acquainted walk-through of the cavernous circa 1922 theater restored to its original grandeur.

"We're still waiting for more apparatus. Parking is at a premium," Herrmann said as fire trucks tried to pull up on busy Bloomfield Avenue, also known as "The Montclair Mile."

Robert McLoughlin, Montclair's chief construction official and a former fire chief, stopped to brief Herrmann.

"They're working on the fire escapes. They're welding. It's safe," McLoughlin said.

And — for the first time — the box office was to open.

"We're giving them a TCO (temporary certificate of occupancy) for the one room," McLoughlin said. "This way they can sell tickets. It's nip and tuck to the end. We're certainly going out of our way at the drop of a hat to give them inspections."

The decibel level rose and fell in successive waves. A churning cement mixer atop a red Mack truck readied concrete for a slab lost to construction. Loads of bottled water and ginger ale were unloaded from a bright red Coca-Cola truck. A white Budweiser truck pulled up immediately behind the other.

The Wellmont's new-hire list was to include seven Montclair police officers, working side jobs on concert nights, as well as a half-dozen firefighters, also working side jobs on the Wellmont payroll.

Neil Feltz, the box office manager who wears a Rutgers University Class of '73 ring and whose résumé includes a long stint at New York City's Beacon Theater, would soon be training his own crew. But outside the theater, Michael Swier of The Bowery Presents, who teamed up with Andy Feltz to bring the Wellmont to life, was coy about the numbers.

The first buyers to line up for tickets — and avoid the online service fee — knew they were making sidewalk history.

Before becoming the first box office patron, Klink had already been, well, sized up.

"Are you the first in line?" Swier asked the Montclair woman as he innocently walked by the booth. A nod later, and tickets in hand, Neil

Feltz told her that her Hanson tickets were free, a honor for being No. 1 on line.

"You're kidding! Oh, wow. Thank you so much," said Klink, who said she will be going to the Nov. 1 concert with her 20-year-old daughter, Elynna Klink.

Next up was John Tobin, but after looking over a seating chart, Tobin faced a delay in getting tickets to see Steely Dan.

"It's cash only," Tobin said. "I live right in town, so it's not a big deal."

Richard Garofalo, a Montclair lawyer who had come to buy Steely Dan tickets as a 47th birthday present for his wife, Cathy, had been talking up the venue as a great alternative to Manhattan. He had to rush around the corner to tap an ATM and quickly ended up back on line, offering advice.

"Up the block, to your left," he instructed those who had credit and debit cards instead of cash.

The Wellmont was directing drivers to 800 spaces: the Bay Street deck for those arriving from Bloomfield eastward, the Walnut Street Train Station surface parking for those arriving from Clifton and Route 3, and the Orange Road deck for those arriving from Verona westward. The $15 spaces will be available from 6 p.m. to 2 a.m. on concert nights.

On Friday, the concertgoers did not hesitate to say what brought them to an old-fashioned ticket booth in the internet age.

"Because I don't want to pay a service fee," said Torre Somma of Lyndhurst, who came to buy tickets to the band Vampire Weekend. "And I'm excited."

Inside the ticket booth, with "wet paint" posters taped to the door and wall, box office manager Neil Feltz was sitting atop an HP computer box. The cash drawer was the pocket of his cold-weather coat, its arm smeared with paint from the fresh coat just applied to the walls.

Joe Cuonze of ticket.com eyed the room in the midst of a construction boom. "I don't see any heating ducts. That's a problem. . . . It's so cold in here."

Neil Feltz pulled the proceeds out of his pocket and readied a shelf for use as a makeshift cash draw.

"Lunch would be good," he said. "We've got all this money."

A coffin containing a skeleton is carried to burial at Mount Hebron Cemetery in Montclair. The remains were left behind in 1926 when the old First Methodist Cemetery was relocated to make way for the old Washington Street YMCA. Photo by Mia Song. Run date, March 13, 2008.

25

AN UNUSUAL FUNERAL

New school forces disinterment

There were no flowers. No mourners with dark glasses. No clergy.

Only Thomas C. Brown, a funeral director dressed in black and stepping out of a shiny Cadillac Fleetwood hearse that had just delivered one of two coffins to Montclair's Mount Hebron Cemetery.

He took a handful of dirt, dropped it atop the coffin at the appropriate time and silently, he said, spoke a solemn prayer and committal.

His unspoken words came from the 23rd psalm, with its well-known opening verse, "The Lord is my shepherd, I shall not want," and from the 121st psalm, which speaks of the Lord's keeping "your going out and coming in . . . forevermore."

"My favorites," said Brown, from Martin's Home for Services in Montclair.

The deceased — believed to be a female — in this case was the intact skeleton of someone who died perhaps a century ago. Her remains were left behind in 1926 when the old First Methodist Cemetery was relocated to make way for the old Washington Street YMCA, which has since been demolished to make way for a new $35 million elementary school.

It took an archaeological dig to unearth the deceased and a court order to disinter the remains, which along with some other bones grouped together in a separate vault were belatedly laid to rest Tuesday with the remains of 85 others moved to Mount Hebron so long ago.

"We don't really get people burying bones. It's a first for me," said Mike DeMaio, the foreman at Mount Hebron Cemetery, who has 36 years of experience.

For Jon Casson, a solemn-sounding cemetery worker, it was also an unusual event.

"This is interesting, I'll tell you, this situation," he said.

The sole interment of the day at Mount Hebron began at 8:30 a.m., when Avery Hill of Maplewood, employed with Suburban Vaults of Newark, arrived with two 2,000-pound concrete vaults.

In a few short hours, he was a member of a funeral procession carrying first the full-sized gray coffin for the intact skeleton and then the child-sized one for the various bones and fragments retrieved largely from the rear yard of the old YMCA.

The deceased, identity unknown, had unintentionally stood in the way of construction crews waiting to build a new 550-pupil school on Montclair's Washington Street, delaying for more than a year a school now expected to open in 2010.

In a Mount Hebron section called C-78, a grave marker lists 85 names of those who died largely between 1838 and 1887 and were reinterred at the cemetery in 1926 to make way for the Washington Street Y. At the time, some remains were simply missed.

Before the disinterment and re-interments, a court order was necessary.

"Any lineal descendants of the deceased cannot be traced as the remains cannot be identified," read the legal brief in the case of "Montclair Board of Education v. Any Living, Lineal Descendants of Any Person or Persons Buried in the Former Burial Ground."

No objections heard, a Superior Court judge in Newark on Feb. 27 signed an order allowing the remains to be removed under the supervision of archaeologists and re-interred under the watchful eyes of a funeral director.

Matthew Tomaso, senior archaeologist with the Cultural Resource Consulting Group, said the remains were removed "very carefully" over three days last week and stored in a secure, climate-controlled location nearby.

The burial didn't come cheap.

The archaeologists cost $25,600, the funeral home's tab was $8,968, and the cemetery's bill came in at $2,550, said Dana Sullivan, the business administrator for Montclair's school district.

Demolition of the old Y, the long-vacant St. Vincent's Nursing Home and Mother Seton Residence — all part of a $4.5 million land acquisition — is now complete for the $35 million school. Today, only hay covers the fence-enclosed lots.

The go-ahead for demolition came after the state Department of Environmental Protection, which had ordered the dig, determined that the "archaeological integrity" of the graveyard had been lost, making it ineligible for historic designation.

The dig uncovered not just remains, but a sizable collection of intact tombstones, now in storage until their destinies can be determined. One showed up during the final removal of the intact skeleton, but Tomaso said he doesn't think it belongs to the deceased.

"We did recover another tombstone," Tomaso said. The name on the stone was Martha Walker.

At the cemetery, her name was among the many listed on the common tombstone of 1926. Date of death: March 26, 1871.

Extras wait for shooting of "Law and Order, Special Victims Unit" filmed Feb. 27 at the Montclair Art Museum. Photo by Mark Dye. Run date, March 4, 2007.

26

HURRY UP AND WAIT

TV show extras hope for a few minutes of fame

Michael Kerns sat squeezed shoulder-to-shoulder with some 150 other movie "extras" or "background" actors, lost in a sea of two-dozen folding tables, trying to read a Stephen King novel.

The clamor inside the cavernous "holding area" for an episode of television's "Law & Order, Special Victims Unit" was deafening. Kerns, a 45-year-old computer programmer from Montclair, had already been in a scene shot earlier.

By mid-afternoon one day last week, a tour bus originating in Manhattan had just unloaded a horde of SAG, or Screen Actors Guild, extras who poured through the glass doors of the gutted space that long ago was the home of Oscar winner Olympia Dukakis' Whole Theater Co. in Montclair.

They waited. They talked. They waited some more. All for a few seconds of fame, perhaps, captured by the cameras in the same frame with Mariska Hargitay (Detective Olivia Benson), and Christopher Meloni (Detective Eliott Stabler.)

"Hopefully, we don't wind up on the cutting-room floor," said Diane

Hirschberg, part of a trio of non-SAG extras from Glen Rock.

Her resume includes the soon-to-be-released feature film "Spider-Man 3" and — her personal favorite — an infomercial with Engelbert Humperdinck for a Time-Life CD called "The Magic of Love."

"That was truly a dream for me," Hirschberg said.

In all, 151 extras or "background" people — some 36 of whom hold the coveted SAG, or Screen Actors Guild, union card — poured into one of New Jersey's hottest film locales for a full-day shoot Tuesday at the Montclair Art Museum, just a few blocks west.

The big crowd was enticed by a casting call put out by New York's Grant Wilfley Casting. The specifications: Well-dressed extras who look like WASPs, or White Anglo-Saxon Protestants, to play congregants of an evangelical mega-church whose minister is a murder suspect.

Some of the extras had their own rap sheets, namely multiple gigs on television's "The Sopranos."

"People saw me!" a black-dress outfitted Jeannie Moorhead of Bloomfield said of getting on "The Sopranos" "Vinny gets whacked" episode.

A sharply tailored Rich Skudera of Cedar Knolls slipped in as an extra at a two-day shoot of "The Sopranos" at Atlantic City's Borgata casino last autumn. In his other life, he's in the commercial real estate business in Roseland. He knows the drill.

"A lot of this is hurry up and wait," he says.

In this life, some extras get extras, some don't.

"It's a two-class system. First class and steerage," said Kevin Murphy, a SAG actor from Manhattan who could pass for onetime presidential candidate John Kerry.

The SAG extras dined first, on hot Mexican dishes prepared by Shooting Stars Catering of Tabernacle in Burlington County. The non-SAGs, as they're called, lined up next for cold cuts.

"The people eating are 'the blessed ones,'" Ron Onorato, a retired educator, said as he waited with fellow non-SAGs Hirschberg and Bonnie McCarthy, who came from Glen Rock. Their recent film "credits" include the Disney flick "Enchanted" and "Bourne Ultimatum," both due out later this year.

The non-SAGs hope for a speaking part, even if it's only a single word. It could lead to coveted SAG card.

"A line in a part, somewhere. Whenever you get someone to say, 'Say this!'" said Anne Plath, a real-estate agent from Bloomfield who recently did some background work for the romantic comedy "Then She Found Me" with Helen Hunt.

In a few minutes, Kerns makes his way to a table for a slice of cheesecake and points to Ron Kidd, an extra who could pass for Vice President Dick Cheney. "Spitting image," Kerns says.

Kidd, an impersonator who carries postcards of his mug alongside Cheney's, said he appeared on the NBC talk show "Late Night with Conan O'Brian."

"Feeding the Iraq report into a paper shedder," said Kidd, displaying that vice presidential smirk.

As the extras are readied for the big scene, the room fills with a lingo all its own.

"All my CSUs and UNIs, there should be about eight of you," shouts Natalie Brown, the 26-year-old "background PA." The call brings up extras robed as crime-scene types or wearing uniforms with NYPD patches.

Brown, a self-described disc-jockey-in-training, stands atop a folding chair and talks location — a mega-church — and plot — the funeral for the minister's veteran son, who was killed in Iraq.

"You idolize your pastor. . . . This is very sad, like family for you guys," she says. "Look sad."

There's a how-to on properly filling out the voucher to get paid. A hand goes up in the crowd.

"The rate for non-SAGs is $75," Brown answers. The base pay for SAGs, says one, is $126, plus overtime, which can add up in a 14-hour shoot.

Up the street at the Montclair Art Museum, whose Leir Hall is set up as the New Souls Church, the "second second assistant director," Kenyon Noble, communicates with the holding area. "Ten minutes. Start loading the buses," says Noble, who grew up in Montclair and Maplewood.

When the "backgrounds" arrive for the filming of "Sin," as the episode is called, Noble ushers them into row of seats, quickly trying to achieve just the right mix of age and sex.

As the filming is about to begin, actor Tim Daly, who plays the Rev. Jeb Curtis, admires an image of himself, arms outstretched, on a large banner with the words, "the truth shall make you free."

The evening gets late. All are seated at the "funeral." The "backgrounds" do their stuff. Eyes are padded with tissues. There are blank stares of grief. In the back are Detectives Stabler and Benson. And for a few fleeting moments, it's the stars — rather than the extras — who are in the background.

Peter R. Greer, center, the headmaster at Montclair Kimberley Academy, is retiring from the school after some 13 years. "My wife said it best, This is the best job I've ever had. And I've had some good jobs before," Greer says. Photo by Andrew Mills. Run date, April 10, 2005.

27

THANK YOU AND FAREWELL, MR. GREER

Headmaster retiring from his best job ever

He's the headmaster with the tony résumé and the signature bow tie.

Peter R. Greer - once a deputy undersecretary of education in the Reagan administration and dean of Boston University's School of Education - is retiring from the private Montclair Kimberley Academy, where he landed after those high-profile roles.

"My wife said it best, This is the best job I've ever had," Greer, 64, said last week from his picture- lined office with its university-style armchairs. "And I've had some good jobs before."

That might be an understatement.

He has rubbed shoulders with chiefs of staff and heads of state, even went up against Sen. Edward Kennedy's softball team when he played with Bennett's Billy Clubs during his stint in D.C.

"He (Kennedy) stacked it with ex-minor league players. They were pros," recalls Greer, whose boss at the time was William J. Bennett, the secretary of education.

The affinity for softball goes back to his days in Portland, Maine, coaching his daughter Rebekah's team, and to his time on the Ipswich (Mass.) Clams. It continues to this day with MKA's girls softball team, the Cougars, who so far this season are 2-0.

"I rarely miss a game. I even go to practices," Greer said.

It is, in fact, one of the things he said he'll miss most when he retires June 17, leaving behind the 1,025-student school after some 13 years and heading with his wife, Terry, to an apartment in Washington, D.C., where they'll be close to their five grandchildren.

Greer, once described by Bennett as an "awfully natty" dresser, looked all the part as he sat in his office at the middle-school campus on Montclair's Valley Road. Over the door is a sign reading, "Character Counts," a reminder of the school's focus on character building and ethics education.

"It's not just something cute and pretty and good PR," Greer said. "We want them to lead, to take people seriously."

This day, as others, many of the students are sporting neck - rather than bow - ties, and aren't above holding the door for the next, trailing arrival. In the hallways between classes, there's the sound of baroque music, broadcast from a CD. It is part of Greer's legacy, an idea he said he picked up from a tough school in Louisiana.

"It calms down the students, and middle-school students can use that," Greer said.

At dismissal, Greer is exchanging greetings. "Gentlemen, you have a good day," he says. A girl passes by and blurts out "Nice bow tie," unleashing the equally signature Greer grin. "The bow tie is doing well today," Greer says.

Also doing well is MKA, whose graduating class so far this year is sending four to Princeton, two each to Harvard and Yale, a total of 20 acceptances to so-called ultra-schools, the product, in part, of a "core works" program that keys in on such things as the Rev. Martin Luther King Jr.'s "Letter from a Birmingham City Jail."

With pride, Greer touts MKA's small class sizes - a dozen to a class in many cases - and a faculty that he said now feels particularly valued. "The faculty said they felt like scholars again," Greer said of his initiatives.

Sometimes they're even star-struck. MKA has attracted visits from Madonna ("She was sweet as anything," Greer recalls), Henry Winkler

("A humble educator," Greer said to describe himself in comparison that day), and even J.K. Rowling, the author of the Harry Potter books (A visit Greer said made his knees knock with awe).

MKA has been Greer's life. "I have no hobbies," said Greer, confessing to waking at night to jot down notes about one idea or another.

George Hrab, who has taught at MKA for 36 years, describes Greer as a driven educator who sets an example by being the first in the office each morning. "The man is an unbelievable worker," Hrab said. "He keeps everybody hopping."

As for Greer, his parents divorced when he was young. His mother married an Army officer. A self- described Army brat, he spent time in dance-hall cloakrooms, deposited there as a child by parents with a love of dancing. "My nestling," he says.

He picked up a love of his own, music from the '40s and '50s. He even sang "In the Still of the Night" at his daughter's wedding. "I just can't understand today's music. I just can't," he says.

From the halls of academia to the corridors of Washington, Greer has enough stories to fill a library, such as the time Bennett asked him to substitute at a political function.

After going through some tight security, itself raising his suspicions, he eyed George Shultz, the secretary of state, and Caspar Weinberger, the secretary of defense. Panic set in. "I thought, 'My God, I'm in the wrong room,'" Greer recalls.

Soon, he was in a receiving line with the blue-suit-wearing Cabinet members, he in khaki slacks and loafers, and who arrives but President Corazon Aquino of the Philippines. "Shultz. Weinberger. Greer," said Greer, pointing to help visualize the lineup.

"Everyone was introduced, and they got to me, and there was this blank stare," Greer recalls. Today, he chalks it up to a Bennett joke.

It was at Boston University where Greer was tapped for the university's first-in-the-nation experiment in running a "troubled" public school system, Chelsea. For a year in the early '90s, he served as interim superintendent of the 3,600-student district.

"They were robbing the kids lunch money," Greer said of schoolhouse gangs, noting that he had only a 10-day suspension at his disposal. But Boston University's no-nonsense leader, President John Silber, he said, advised a tough strategy, saying the university's lawyers could hold off any legal challenges by irate parents. "Expel them," Greer said of the mandate.

And it was at a Boston University commencement that Greer said he heard his most powerful speech - from Fred Rogers of television's "Mr. Rogers' Neighborhood." Thousands of graduates packed the university's field. "They were raucous," he said.

Then Rogers appeared. "He got up and said, 'Would you like to sing a song?'" Greer recalls. Soon, the crowd was: "It's a beautiful day in the neighborhood, a beautiful day in the neighborhood." Today, Greer has it on tape. "I use it in the ethics program, to show self-control and respect," Greer said.

As for retirement, Greer is considering writing a book, tentatively titled "Stumbling Through Education." "I certainly didn't come from Princeton," said Greer, who picked up his undergraduate and master's degrees at the University of New Hampshire and his doctorate at Boston University.

Greer - who over the years has endured "teasing" for being a Republican in a Democratic hotbed, a Red Sox fan in Yankee territory - worries about the endurance of something else: MKA's piped-in baroque music.

"They say one second after I leave, they'll put rap on," Greer said. "They say, 'The moment you're gone, Greer.'"

THE ENVIRONS
Run date, Feb. 10, 2002

28

CLIFTON SECTION LOVES ITS NEIGHBOR

Call it "The other Montclair." On the town's northern edge is Clifton, a Passaic County city that long ago capitalized on its proximity to its fashionable Essex County neighbor.

The neighborhood there is called Montclair Heights. A mid-1950s development of split-level homes is called Montclair Vista. Just within the city's border is the Montclair Beach Club. The Upper Montclair Country Club isn't even close. It's way inside Clifton's borders, paying $263,244 in taxes to New Jersey's 11th largest city.

The Clifton, or rather Montclair Heights, residents who live near Valley Road actually have return address labels that say "Upper Montclair," simply because they share a ZIP code - 07043 - and a post office abutting a Starbucks in Upper Montclair.

"I pay taxes in Clifton but live in Upper Montclair," says Helen Suchanek, who for 27 years has lived on McCosh Road along Clifton's far western border, a stone's throw from Montclair State University.

This is about perception, especially important in real estate circles, and class and business ties that date back decades. In some ways, Montclair Heights is to Clifton what Short Hills is to Millburn, what Pompton Plains is to Pequannock, even what Upper Montclair is to Montclair.

Roger Cole is a living piece of the then and now.

He grew up on Montclair Heights' Woodlawn Avenue, a steeply sloped street with expansive ranches reaching up to McCosh Road. Before Woodlawn Avenue came through, this sliver of Clifton was out of reach, possibly part of the reason Upper Montclair delivered the mail.

He is also the owner of the Montclair Beach Club, third generation, and actually moved to Montclair proper himself in 1994. His swimming club - there's really no beach - covers 5.24 acres and pays $40,180 in taxes to Clifton. His grandfather started the place in 1931 as the "Montclair Swimming Pool."

"The line was a little more vague then," he said of the boundary between

Montclair and Clifton along Grove Street, a main corridor for Montclair commuters heading to eastbound Route 3.

"Montclair is really our drawing card," said the now 50-year-old Cole, who says he has a waiting list for the maximum 550 family membership slots.

Across the street is MontClift Service Center, owned by Ray Sikorsky Sr. "He's the last (street) number, I'm the next to last," Sikorsky says of their Clifton addresses.

"All my amenities I get from Essex County, and I pay taxes in Clifton," which are about half what he would pay in Montclair, Sikorsky said.

Property taxes do play a role. In Clifton's Montclair Heights section, a five-bedroom Colonial listed at $489,900 by Burgdorff Realtors' Montclair office has a tax bill of about $8,400. A comparable property in Montclair would generate a tax bill of about $13,000 or more, said Ruth Camooso of Burgdorff, the listing agent.

Her take on who the buyer will be: a large family, someone who might commute into Manhattan, perhaps a relocation. This property, too, she says has some of the appeal of Montclair's.

"They have the charm of some of the older homes," she says. "The construction is excellent - hardwood floors, very good, large rooms."

The biggest selling point: "You can go into Montclair for shopping and dining, and you pay Clifton taxes."

She won't get any argument from Kenneth Hauser of Weichert's Clifton office.

"The Montclair Heights section is very hot," says Hauser, who pegs the price range at $300,000 to $600,000. "It's got the finest homes. It's got executive-style homes to mid-range homes. It's close to Montclair. Taxes are good."

There's perception at work too.

Some New Jersey towns - and real estate interests - have managed to carve out separate identities for upscale neighborhoods in towns whose names don't quite have that certain cache. It's even at work inside Montclair, with house-hunters coming in and asking specifically for Upper Montclair over simply Montclair.

"They think Upper Montclair is the upper end of the price range," says Denise Riordan of Schweppe & Co. Realtors of Upper Montclair, noting pricier and much larger properties in Montclair's Estate section to the south and the mansion row of Upper Mountain Avenue. "It's just somebody drew a line at Watchung (Avenue), and one is 07042 and one is 07043."

The line in Montclair Heights is perhaps as strong, but not impregnable.

Victoria Schuckman grew up in Clifton's Montclair Heights, eventually becoming a school librarian in Montclair. These days, she's running Chelsea Square, a store on Upper Montclair's Valley Road.

Hers is also a story of the economic and social pull of Montclair in that far western corner of 12-square-mile Clifton, twice the size of its Essex neighbor. She now lives in Montclair.

"When I was growing up, we'd shop here, go to the movies . . . skate at the Montclair Rink," Schuckman says. "Clifton doesn't really have a town center. They have Main Avenue, but that was far away."

She knows a lot of her customers hail from Montclair Heights. "I always recognize them from the phone numbers or the street addresses because I grew up there."

If anything, Montclair's newest amenity, Midtown Direct train service to Manhattan, will have another lasting impact this spring in Montclair Heights, says Schweppe's Riordan.

"It's a nice area, very much like Montclair," she said. "And it's close to the train."

Run Date, Nov. 28, 2001

29

OUT OF THIS WORLD, BUT CLOSE TO HOME

Mark Kelly couldn't help stopping by the old neighborhood.

"I even knocked on the door once," Kelly said of the boyhood home he left about 14 years ago on West Orange's Greenwood Avenue. No. 9 to be exact. "The lady wouldn't let me in," he said of the "new" homeowners.

Not quite the reception you might expect when an astronaut - one about to pilot the shuttle Endeavour on an 11-day mission to the international space station set for a 7:41 p.m. launch tomorrow- comes to your front door.

Still, Kelly did chat on the stoop, surmising his impromptu visit from Houston a couple years ago didn't coincide with the homeowners' attention to housekeeping detail. He understands.

Perhaps that's because this decorated pilot, this veteran of 39 combat missions in Desert Storm, this man who safely put F-18s and the like on the deck of aircraft carriers at least 375 times, had a humble start: stomping through a neighbor's flower garden, delivering pizza for Panzone's on Long Beach Island, and trekking off to see the Rocky Horror Picture Show at the Rockaway Mall.

"Rough and tumble. They liked to play," recalls Lucy Broomall, who still lives next door, at No. 11 Greenwood, to the house where police officers Richard and Patricia Kelly raised their twin sons, Mark and Scott, before moving to Florida in 1987. "Very active," Broomall said of the boys.

Richard Kelly admits to giving his twins more freedom than some were comfortable with, including the boys' grandparents, even letting them loose on his docked shore boat during their early teens one summer - unsupervised.

"We raised them a little different than most people," he said. "In fact, we got some heat for it." It was all about what Richard Kelly calls the code. "We had trust in them, that was the main thing," he said. "You told us the truth, no problem. We had a code. We talked about it once. We don't nag."

He recalls the flower-stomping episode: "Somehow or other, he tore up the woman's flowers across the street. She came over to the house and said, 'One of your sons did it.'"

That's when Mark spoke. "I did it," his father recalls the boy saying. He was instructed to go over and replant the flowers. "Boy, his head was hanging." The message, he said, was this: "Be an honorable person."

He has no regrets, having raised not one but two astronauts. Mark's brother, Scott, went aloft on Discovery in 1999. Though Mark follows two years after his brother's flight, their father said his sons don't have a sibling rivalry.

"Only over girls, when they were in their teens," Richard Kelly said, "but not with each other. And they were taught to never give up on anything. If you can't get in the front door, get in the back door, there's always a way."

Should the 107th shuttle mission - the 12th to visit the space station - launch on schedule, Robin McCann will be at Kennedy Space Center in Cape Canaveral, Fla. She's part of a horde of West Orange's own who have been invited to witness the launch.

And while NASA officials say there have been no specific threats against the shuttle, security is tighter than ever as a result of the Sept. 11 terrorists attacks.

McCann is an alumnus of Mountain High School, Class of 1982, as were the Kellys. They've kept in touch all these years. She's now married with two young children in Fairfield. It is McCann who recalls the trip to see the Rocky Horror Picture Show.

In the years after high school, Mark sent postcards, even a poster of a jet he was flying. "I always got interesting things in the mail." She remembers his stint on the swim team and the honor society. She even recalls him saying he'd be an astronaut someday.

"I thought they were both going to be doctors," she said of the twins. "I think they were even in the Future Physicians Club, and it was in our senior year that Mark said, 'I'm going to be an astronaut.' But we didn't believe him."

Mark Kelly said he'll look for some sort of message to send back home to New Jersey folks. "I'll try to get some pictures of New Jersey when I'm in space," he said, "if I have the time. We get pretty busy."

His payload will include the Expedition Four crew he'll help get to the space station and 6,000 postcard-sized U.S. flags that upon their return will be mounted and presented to families of the victims of terrorists attacks in New York, Washington and Pennsylvania. They also are carrying two full-sized U.S. flags that were recovered from the ruins at the World Trade

Center and the Pentagon.

And his payload includes some mementos from West Orange's Thomas Edison laboratories, including a Edison Blue Amberol wax cylinder record dating from 1913 and titled "Come, Josephine, in My Flying Machine."

Back on Greenwood Avenue, life has changed since the early days of space flight. Maria Newman and her family have lived on the street only a few years. On Monday, her children, Robert, 4, and Julianne, 2, piloted plastic cars in the driveway.

Newman alerted her children that they lived across the street and a few doors down from the boyhood home of an astronaut, and reminded them of astronaut masks and jet packs they created in school the year before. Do you know who lived across the street? she asked her children. The response was decidedly Earth-centered.

"I live across the street from Andrew," young Robert said of his own boyhood friend.

Run date, Nov. 28, 2001

30

YES, IT'S TRUE: TOM CRUISE SLEPT HERE
Short street in Glen Ridge has history

It was long before 1986's "Top Gun," even before the career-launching blockbuster movie "Risky Business." But Tom Cruise, the toothy box-office star, once lived here.

Washington Street, Glen Ridge, is an east-to-west roadway in the heart of the small borough's South End. When he wasn't wrestling at Glen Ridge High or playing the role of Nathan Detroit in the school production of "Guys and Dolls," Cruise came home to a circa 1890 Queen Anne with the octagonal towers.

Gary Potter, who grew up on nearby Hawthorne Avenue, once rang the doorbell on Halloweens past.

"He always handed out the candy," said Potter, who is pictured with Cruise and the rest of the concert choir in Glen Ridge High's 1980 yearbook, called the "glenalog." He was a freshman, Cruise a senior. "The first time I ever saw that picture was on TV one night while I was watching a documentary on Tommy," he said.

Today, the star's onetime home belongs to Marie O'Neil, who has an attic memento in the form of an old box with the lettering "Tom's model airplanes," the toy aircraft long since gone.

"I use to get mail with his name on it quite often," said O'Neil, who years ago first rented the house from Norma and Lars Beene, as had the future star's family before her, and then wound up buying it a decade ago.

One time, a particularly passionate fan came along.

"She was up from Florida, and I wasn't home, thank goodness," said O'Neil as she detailed the note's content. "I am here for the weekend," it read. "I will do anything if you please let me walk through the house."

But the street is more than just the boyhood home of a big Hollywood box-office draw. Washington Street, according to historical records, was once the abode of William Bradbury, who wrote the music for such famed hymns as "Jesus Loves Me," "Savior, Like a Shepherd Lead Us" and "Just As I Am."

All of which makes Janit London a little unnerved.

"That's interesting because I'm a songwriter," said London, who moved into Bradbury's pre-1856 home in 1999. What's even more interesting is the organ music she swears she hears while in the downstairs shower.

"This morning," she said was when she last heard the organ music. "I really haven't known what to make of it."

After a few years, Bradbury sold the house to Thomas Wyckoff Langstroth, who was engaged in the manufacture of locks for prisons and banks and was the inventor of the round latchkey lock.

He went on to serve on Bloomfield's governing body (Glen Ridge wasn't separated from Bloomfield until 1895) and the state Assembly, finally dying quietly at home in 1892, according to an obituary in The Bloomfield Citizen.

Since London's arrival, she said, she has rebuilt the porch to match an 1895 photo of the Bradbury House, one she found at the Glen Ridge Library. She also put to use a set of French doors she discovered in the basement. There might be more treasures about.

A woman who once lived in the house, she said, was in town for her high school reunion and shared a story with her. "She told me her father used to bury garbage in the yard," London said. Somewhere under the house, she was told, a Tiffany-style lamp supposedly is yet to come to light.

"I haven't really found the time," she said of locating it.

London's house is on the lower, eastern end of Washington, not far from a site that might explain how the street got its name.

At Washington Street and Ashland Avenue, just over the Bloomfield border, is a faded sign noting the location of Col. Thomas Cadmus' circa 1763 house, stones of which were used in the building with the impressive columns sitting there today.

George Washington stopped at the home after the Battle of Monmouth, on his way to New York state, the plaque reads.

Travel westward, up past the street's center at Ridgewood Avenue, and history is still being written, in the home of author Neil Baldwin.

The writer's works include 2002's "Henry Ford and the Jews: The Mass Production of Hate," 2001's "Edison: Inventing the Century" and 2005's "The American Revelation: Ten Ideals that Shaped Our Country from the Puritans to the Cold War."

The prolific writer's wife is Roberta Baldwin, who by nature of her real estate license gives Washington Street the Realtor's seal of approval.

"Needless to say, I see hundreds of houses a year," said Baldwin, who use to live off Montclair's Watchung Avenue. "I stepped into the foyer of this house and I just knew it. . . . A one-of-a-kind, and it has such a huge yard, almost a half-acre. . . . When you compare it to our 50-by-100 lot in Upper Montclair, I couldn't resist."

Washington Street, she said, is a little busier than other roads, but it has that "South Ender — capital S, capital E — camaraderie."

One of the more recent sales on the street was a circa 1903 four-bedroom, which sold last year for $781,500. "It was one of those great houses," said Paige Schmidt of Rhodes Van Note Realtors. "The yard was 200 feet deep."

It was 25 years ago when, fresh from Glen Ridge, Cruise got his big break in 1981's "Endless Love," playing Billy in a drama starring Brooke Shields, followed the same year with the role of David Shawn in "Taps."

But at home in Glen Ridge, he went by his real name: Thomas C. Mapother IV. He even went to the orthodontist, where Roberta Baldwin on a visit with her son learned of the hesitant patient.

"Tommy never wanted his teeth touched, and of course later on, he had them capped," she said.

Greg Fruhman of Clifton, a fan of comic actor Eddie Bracken, looks through old scripts and other memorabilia during estate sale in Bracken's Glen Ridge home. Memorabilia on sale, right, included sheet music and a photo of Bracken with dancer Donald O'Connor in "The Sunshine Boys." Photos by Christopher Barth. Run date, July 22, 2003.

31

ESTATE SALE OFFERS A RARE GLIMPSE
Momentos of actor Eddie Bracken

The classified ad was headlined simply "ESTATE SALE" and gave the address of a grand Glen Ridge Victorian house.

But this was more than a sale for antique-lovers and bargain-hunters. It was a glimpse into the life of Eddie Bracken, a headliner of stage and screen, and a chance to own a piece of his legacy for a few dollars - or a few hundred.

It brought out the likes of Jim Mahon, who had been in Bracken's home before, in the company of another star, Joyce Randolph, aka Trixie Norton from TV's "The Honeymooners." That get-together was some 14 months ago.

Now Mahon was picking through some autographed books spread out on a table on the second floor of Bracken's home. In his hands, he held a copy - priced at $40 - of "Preston Sturges by Preston Sturges," signed by the late director's widow and carrying this inscription: "Dear Eddie: A very important part of your life and my life too, Sandy."

Sturges, the man who directed Bracken in such film classics as "Hail the Conquering Hero" and "The Miracle of Morgan's Creek," died long ago. Bracken, at 87, died in November, just weeks after his wife of 62 years, and the estate sale was perhaps the final curtain.

"I live right down the street," said Mahon, a psychoanalyst with a practice in Montclair. How did he come to know "Trixie"? "From hanging out at Sardies for years and years."

Downstairs in the kitchen, Randi Blauth had just made a love-at-first-sight decision, opting to pay $2 for a ceramic sign reading "WC" on the powder room door. "It's English. It's water closet."

Yet she knew the significance of the moment. "It's a sad but neat experience," she said of the sale, which on Friday and Saturday brought out crowds to look - and perhaps buy - a small piece of Bracken's life.

Entering the large vestibule, there was a Seth Thomas banjo clock, priced at $45. An upright piano, priced at $400. An abundance of furnishings and paintings, some by his daughter Susan, one of his five grown children, and even one by Bracken himself, for $950.

Up the stairs, past the small pieces of green, yellow and orange tape intended to keep the unfamiliar from tripping, past the "Watch Your Step" sign, stood a door to what was described as Bracken's study.

There, a line extended down the hallway, pass the master bedroom with its deep blue wallpaper punctuated with small red roses on green stems. Inside, past the sign reading "Limit 3 people in this room, Thank you," stood Suzanne Ambrosio.

She was among the more than a dozen people working with Mary Wood Estate and House Sales of Montclair and arguably had the day's most sought-after memorabilia.

There was the "Home Alone 2, Lost in New York" package, with scripts and a signed picture of child star Macaulay Culkin. "Dear Eddie: Nice working with you. Your friend, Macaulay Culkin, aka Mack." It was priced at $50.

There was the trophy Bracken received when he was inducted into the National Broadcasters Hall of Fame. Price tag: $25. There was even a framed picture of Bracken white-water rafting with his family, for $10.

"He kept everything," Ambrosio said. "It was a lot of fun to go through it, read the letters, piece it together," she said of the "prep work" for the estate sale.

In the next room, where Mahon had been eyeing the autographed books, Erma Etergino, one of Ambrosio's co-workers, said it's a delicate process.

"We go through them very carefully," she said.

Downstairs, Kathy Tyahla of Clifton, who minutes before had been eyeing the "Home Alone 2" lot, stood on a line 15 deep, waiting to pay Mary Wood at the front door. Instead, she held a lot from the 1991 film "Oscar," starring Sylvester Stallone. It included a personal letter director John Landis wrote to Bracken.

"That was a nice find," she said of her $30 purchase, attracting the attention of Melissa Schaffer of Montclair.

"That is very amazing, so cool," Schaffer said of the Landis note.

By the end of Saturday, any unsold items - about 10 percent of the house's contents - were destined for a charity called "Angel Street," whose Manhattan shop uses the proceeds to fund rehabilitation programs, Wood said.

Back in the kitchen, where she had grabbed the "WC" sign, Blauth spoke affectionately of the late actor. Blauth, a Glen Ridge teacher, had taught Bracken's grandson in middle school.

Once, wanting a special surprise for her god-daughter's 16th birthday, she asked Bracken's daughter if she could land tickets to the sold-out musical Carousel at the Paper Mill Playhouse in Millburn, where Bracken frequently performed. The box office soon called, saying "Mr. Bracken" had arranged for the tickets, she said.

"That was his last show," she said of his role as an endearing starkeeper in "Carousel." "He was an angel."

Maria Pepe of Hoboken speaks at the Yogi Berra Museum. In 1972, Maria Pepe played Little League for the Hoboken Young Democrats. That was before the organization's national headquarters threatened to revoke the team's charter for breaking its ban on girls. Photos by Robert Sciarrino. Run date, May 6, 2005.

32

IT TOOK A HOBOKEN GIRL TO STRIKE OUT LITTLE LEAGUE'S BAN

They took away her uniform in 1972

In the annals of baseball history, pioneers are rare.

Jackie Robinson broke the color barrier in Major League Baseball. Curt Flood opened the door to free agency and its eye-popping salaries.

And Maria Pepe shattered the gender barrier in Little League.

For three games in 1972, Pepe - then a 12-year-old with a deep passion for the game and a mean fastball - donned the colors of the Hoboken "Young Democrats" and stepped out of the dugout in the so-called "Birthplace of Baseball."

Then it was over.

"I think the hardest part was when they took my uniform away," Pepe said yesterday, her voice breaking as she recalled that dark moment in her Hoboken childhood. "I didn't feel I was doing anything harmful."

Her Little League career didn't last long, but it propelled a "shy kid" into the national limelight and forever changed the role of girls in the national pastime.

"They would ask me, 'Why do you want to play baseball?' I still remember the headlines: 'Maria Pepe kicked off team.'"

Thirty-two years and 5 million female Little Leaguers later, Pepe told her pioneering story yesterday to a room full of Montclair seventh-graders at the Yogi Berra Museum & Learning Center on the campus of Montclair State University.

"Part of my healing," she said of one of her rare public appearances.

In 1972, there were no girls softball teams. Pepe's friends told their Little League coach, Jimmy Farina, that there was a girl who could not only pitch, but hit and field, too.

"He said, 'Why aren't you signing up?'" she remembered. "'Because I'm a girl,'" was the response. "He said, 'Can you play?'"

Play she could, beating out a crop of boys and securing a spot as a starting pitcher and left fielder.

Soon, the letter came from the Little League's national headquarters, threatening to revoke the team's charter for breaking the league's ban on girls. After getting the news from the coach, Pepe turned in her uniform. The case attracted national attention and the Yankees honored her and her family with a special day at Yankee Stadium.

It also attracted some unwelcome attention.

She told of riding in an elevator in the 10-story Hoboken apartment building her family lived in when she was confronted by a "gentleman" with an opinion. "He was really yelling at me in the elevator, 'You're causing all this trouble in town,'" she recalled. "I'd never tell anybody."

Soon, the National Organization for Women approached her family about championing her cause, and they agreed. It would take two years - by then Pepe was too old for Little League - but the courts sided with her.

"The institution of Little League is as American as the hot dog and apple pie," Sylvia Pressler, then a hearing examiner for the state Division of Civil Rights, said in her ruling. "There is no reason that part of Americana should be withheld from girls." The ruling was later upheld in Superior Court, and the dugout gates were opened.

Her brief Little League career was enough to make ESPN's Top 10 list of the greatest moments in U.S. women's sports history, coming in at No. 5.

Pepe said she has come "full circle," attending last year's Little League World Series in Williamsport, Pa. There, she got to meet Creighton Hale, who as president of the Little League had appeared in court to oppose girls playing in the league.

"When he shook my hand, he said, 'I just wanted to say my granddaughter plays.' . . . It was very heart-warming."

Yesterday, she was like a kid again, briefly getting to meet the museum's namesake, Yankees great Yogi Berra, and snapping a picture of her "YD" uniform-clad self in the museum's "Jersey Girls" display, as well as the field at the adjoining stadium. "It brings back a lot of memories." She proudly notes she still has all her old baseball cards.

After Little League, Pepe went on to play basketball and softball in high school and varsity baseball at St. Peter's College in Jersey City.

Today, at 45, she still calls Hoboken home and is a CPA and controller at Hackensack University Medical Center. She occasionally plays in company games pitting managers against administrators, sometimes batting against hospital CEO John Ferguson.

"I did get a good hit off of him," she said.

She doesn't discount the coming of a day when there will be a professional women's baseball league. "Hopefully I'll be young enough I can play."

Yet Pepe, who said she tends to be quiet and sentimental about her story, clearly enjoyed speaking with the seventh-graders from Montclair's Renaissance School. She, too, opened the eyes of some of the girls who today are doing what she was forbidden to do.

"It inspires me to keep going on with baseball," said Maggie Regan, a 13-year-old who plays second base with the Renaissance Raptors.

It also got Ava Kravitz thinking.

"I want to know if there's a Montclair baseball girls league," said the 12-year-old first baseman for The Sparks. "I think it's only softball."

As for Pepe, even today she wouldn't necessarily be a good fit for softball. "I could never windmill pitch. I just never could get that rhythm."

Mark Rudd, a one-time member of the Weather Underground, today teaches at a community college. Photos by David Fenton/ITVS. Run date, March 19, 2004.

33

NOTES FROM THE UNDERGROUND
60s radical revisits his roots

Mark Rudd remembers growing up in a typical upper-middle-class household in Maplewood.

He was a Boy Scout. He went to Hebrew School. At Columbia High School in the early 1960s, he belonged to the electronics club and played on the soccer team.

"I was a nice Jewish boy in the suburbs," said Rudd, now 56.

Barbara Schwartz Cowen remembers those days, too.

"He was the first guy I ever dated," said Cowen, recalling that she was about 14 and, as best she can remember, accompanied Rudd to a middle school dance. "Mark was very smart, very funny . . . but you know, he just went his own way," Cowen said.

Rudd's childhood friend in the Class of 1965 wouldn't realize just how far afield he had gone until the shock of watching a television newscast a few years later.

Mark Rudd had become a revolutionary, the leader of the famous 1968 student occupation and strike at New York's Columbia University and soon-to-be fugitive of the Weather Underground.

Now, 36 years later, Rudd will talk of his radical past when he comes to the New Jersey premiere of the Academy Award-nominated documentary

"The Weather Underground," to be shown at 7:30 p.m. tomorrow at the JCC Ross Family Campus on West Orange's Northfield Avenue.

"I think Mark was looking for an opportunity to come back home and appear in his own community, where he grew up," said Herbert Ford, who is the chair of the New Jersey Jewish Film Festival.

Today, Rudd is the most infamous of Columbia High's roster of famous grads, who have included Grammy winner Lauryn Hill, Oscar-nominated actress Elisabeth Shue and actor Roy Scheider of the classic 1975 summer flick "Jaws."

But aside from Rudd's starring roles in the evening news footage of the 1960s and 1970s, this full-length film features his reflections of the times, interspersed with clips of the Vietnam War's grimmest images.

There's the footage of the Saigon street execution of a Vietcong prisoner in 1968, immediately followed by Rudd's commentary: "Our country was murdering millions of people. This revelation was more than we could handle."

Film clips of newscaster Walter Cronkite follow and the then-familiar body count projected on the TV screen, at that point 30,057. There's an image of the Rev. Martin Luther King Jr. speaking of the "evil, unjust war," and soon the footage of a Vietnamese girl fleeing a napalm attack in 1973. Again the camera shifts to Rudd. "'Bring the War Home' was our slogan," Rudd said. And they did.

The Weather Underground, mostly middle-class students, set off a series of bombs, choosing targets that were politically symbolic, including the home of a New York City judge, a Pentagon lavatory and a New York State Department of Corrections facility. Each time, the group called in a bomb threat well before the explosion, allowing the buildings to be evacuated so no one would be hurt.

Today, Rudd lives a quiet life teaching what he describes as "low-level math" at a community college in Albuquerque, N.M., something he has done for 24 years now. He has two grown children, Paul, 29, and Elena, 25, who is to be married next month in San Diego.

"I am a person who lives right now, in the present. My career is not in the past," Rudd said.

But he does remember his childhood in New Jersey.

His grandmother ran a candy store in Newark at 15th Avenue and 11th Street, he said, and he would take the bus down South Orange Avenue to visit. He went to Maplewood's Jefferson School and Maplewood Junior High School, the son of an Army Reserve officer who went into the real estate business managing apartments in Elizabeth and Newark.

In his high school yearbook picture, he is sporting a jacket and tie and a smile, but that wasn't necessarily a reflection of his mood. "I was not happy in high school," he said last week. But he was busy, writing a column for the student newspaper, the Columbian.

In a post-election column headlined "Rally 'Round The Ruins," Rudd writes of the end of a "torturous 10-week nightmare," namely the Johnson-Goldwater campaign in 1964, and his affection for Johnson's running mate, Hubert Humphrey.

He concludes with this: "Politics has been shown to be not only compromising, but immoral. This is a bad time for this revelation."

There are hints of his political bend in the text accompanying his high school picture: "Government finds it roots in anarchy" . . . "not facts, ideas, man, ideas" . . . "oblivious, walking along the road to greatness."

"He was hanging around with the intellectual crowd," Cowen recalls. "From what I understand, he just went crazy."

Rudd admits as much, speaking in the film of the "terrible, demented logic" that took him and the Students for a Democratic Society from perpetrators of civil disobedience to advocates of a violent overthrow of the U.S. government.

These days, Rudd comes to New Jersey a few times a year, visiting his older brother, David, in Morristown, and his 92-year-old mother in Whippany. Until 2001, the home at 75 Maplewood Ave. was the Rudds'.

It was an unsettling time during the seven-plus years Rudd was an FBI fugitive. Rudd never served any jail time. Federal charges were dropped in 1973, and he pleaded down state charges in New York and Illinois to misdemeanor offenses. Today in New Mexico, Rudd is active in his teachers union and local environmental and peace issues. He is appreciative of "The Weather Underground" film.

"Very few people in their middle age have a chance to look at themselves when they were kids and discuss it with people," he said last week. "It's a very fascinating experience, and I learned a lot. . . . I think the filmmakers really gave me a terrific gift."

If there's any judgment, it's not coming from his brother.

"I don't judge other people," said David Rudd, adding that many of the radicals depicted in the film are Jewish and might have been influenced by the "heal the world" doctrine of the faith.

"These are people who felt very strongly about righting the world, correcting a wrong," he said.

As for Mark Rudd, he wouldn't venture into what his 20-something children think of their father's radical exploits.

"Too complicated. I don't want to get into it," he said. "Let's just say they're living their own lives, which I think is fabulous, which is exactly the way it should be."

Herb Degan of Cedar Grove, who from 1937 until 1941 was the CBS radio announcer for the Saturday afternoon program "Matinee at the Meadowbrook," will reprise his role for the "Hollywood Canteen" concert featuring the Glenn Miller Orchestra. Photo by Jerry McCrea. Run date, July 7, 2003.

34

THE JOINT'S GONNA JUMP AGAIN

A swinging gala's on tap for the old Meadowbrook

It was the big-band era, and through the magic of radio, people all over the country would hear these familiar words: "Coming to you from Frank Dailey's Meadowbrook, Route 23, the Pompton Turnpike in Cedar Grove, N.J."

What came next into American living rooms (and perhaps the back seat of the old family Plymouth) were the sounds of Glenn Miller, Tommy Dorsey and Frank Sinatra. The Meadowbrook was big enough to get them all, and for the World War II generation, it was the place to go to see them live.

But, as always, things changed. The big bands came and went, and the Meadowbrook became a dinner-theater in the 1960s and then a disco in the 1980s. Then it fell silent, and then into disrepair.

Now one man is bringing back the glory days of the Meadowbrook, if just for one night. Mike Grabas, who spends his Sundays visiting hospitalized veterans, is creating a "Hollywood Canteen" night at the Meadowbrook on Aug. 16 to benefit the men he so admires.

"A lot of them, actually 90 percent of them, are in wheelchairs, some in fetal positions. Basically, they're in their final battle," said Grabas, 46, the chairman of the veterans committee of Cedar Grove Elks Lodge No. 2237.

The Meadowbrook has been renovated by its new owner, Sts. Kiril & Metodij Macedonian Orthodox Church, and is ready to host the special night, headlined by the Glenn Miller Orchestra.

Grabas got the idea while visiting the thinning ranks of World War II veterans at the Lyons Veterans Hospital in Somerset County - men of his parents' generation.

"I grew up with World War II stories," said Grabas, whose mother, Betty, would take him on drives around Cedar Grove, pointing out homes of soldiers who didn't come back.

Grabas - whose PT Cruiser sports flags from the various branches of the armed services but who never served in the military - said the gala is intended to raise as much as $15,000.

The money will go to his Elks Lodge, which will use it to help raise the spirits of hospitalized veterans with picnics and entertainment, such as the three-woman, Andrews Sisters-style USO troupe that will open for the Glenn Miller Orchestra at the show.

Grabas hopes the event will draw about 700 people paying $45 each for a night of dancing - buffet and beer included.

"A lot of people want to see what the Meadowbrook looked like," said Grabas, who works at a West Caldwell supermarket. "It will bring back a lot of memories, a lot of memories."

It will for Herb Degan, who from 1937 until 1941 was the CBS radio announcer for the Saturday afternoon program "Matinee at the Meadowbrook" before heading overseas as a B-17 pilot flying some 25 missions.

"It looks pretty much like it was," he said last week from the balcony overlooking the 40-by-100-foot dance floor. It was the first time he'd set foot in the place since 1947.

"You've done a beautiful job with it," said the 86-year-old Degan, turning to the Rev. Slobodan Petkovski, whose congregation uses the newly refurbished hall for brunches and dances for its 600 families.

Its sanctuary is still under construction next door to the old Meadowbrook, which the church purchased in 1994 and renovated with new woodwork and carpeting. The church has extended invitations to the clergy of Cedar Grove to come to the "Hollywood Canteen" as a way to get to know the community.

"We stumbled across it, actually," Zvonko Veskov, a member of the church committee, said of the old Meadowbrook.

Back in the big-band era, it was a destination.

The Meadowbrook - started by Frank Dailey's Meadowbrook Syncopators in the 1930s - was such a cultural icon that Charlie Barnet penned a tune called "Pompton Turnpike," whose lyrics noted that the hall's "music interlude puts you right in the mood." Even the famed Tokyo Rose, the Japanese radio propaganda queen, once falsely reported that the Meadowbrook burned down, hoping to demoralize the troops.

"I don't think there was a finer tribute," said Philip Edward Jaeger, the author of "Cedar Grove," one of Arcadia Publishing's Images of America series.

The place holds special memories for Marietta Rhatican, who was Dailey's nighttime secretary starting around 1950. Dailey, she said, was so touched by a letter from GIs thanking him for his dance club's music that he had it enlarged and framed in his office.

"He was a terrific guy, a very, very nice man," she said of the violin-playing Dailey, who died in the early 1950s after being stricken with a heart attack during a gala event for RCA.

"That was (at) the end of the big-band era," said Rhatican, who now lives in Berkeley Heights. "He was still having Tommy and Jimmy Dorsey. They were not drawing the way they had been."

Through all the changes, dinner-theater to disco, the Meadowbrook was always best remembered as the place Dailey put on the map when the big bands were in full swing.

"It's possibly haunted by Frank Dailey," Grabas said while motioning to the late violinist's old office off the bar on the second-floor balcony. "In the disco days, a couple guys came in and heard a violin playing. That I don't believe."

With natural gas costs on the rise, Glen Ridge is looking at cheaper ways to keep its 667 gas lamps — like this one on Lorraine Street — illuminated. Photo by Scott Lituchy. Run date, April 2, 2006.

35

RUNNING ON EMPTY

Glen Ridge basks in costly gaslight

The small-town charm here is punctuated on every street corner by a classic gas lamp with an eternal flame. It is so central to Glen Ridge, ranked as New Jersey's most historic town, that few can imagine suburban life without it.

But the natural gas that powers those 667 lamps — 24 hours a day, seven days a week — has become as painful as gassing up the SUV with $2.39-a-gallon petrol.

"The cost of gas lamps has been one of the biggest cost drivers (percentage-wise) in our budget, rising 180 percent since 1999," said Michael Rohal, Glen Ridge's borough manager. Mayor Carl Bergmanson put it this way: "It's a real budget buster."

Today, the flickering lights cost $35.31 a year for every man, woman and child in this small sliver of a town with 7,123 people. In 1999, the little flames cost $90,490 to run. Last year, it was $251,544, and so far this year, the cost is running 17 percent ahead of just a year ago.

Not that anyone would consider retiring the hallmark lamps, images of which appear on everything from Friends of the Library tote bags to Glen Ridge Historical Society postcards to the community's official seal.

"It's a big number, but they really identify the town," Prudence Borland, a longtime Glen Ridger, said while en route to the library late one afternoon. "For $3 a month, I'll hang tight. I'll pay my share."

The American gas lamp, and Glen Ridge's in particular, has a storied history.

In 1961, the Saturday Evening Post ran an article noting that Glen Ridge, South Orange and East Orange were about the only New York suburbs with the "archaic distinction" of having gaslights. Just a few years earlier, in the late 1950s, newspaper headlines were marking their demise in one of those places: "Old Gas Street Lamps Fading As East Orange Goes Electric."

By 1976, the New Jersey Board of Public Utilities had branded gas street lighting "an economic misuse" of a natural resource in short supply.

Glen Ridge, meanwhile, looked at converting the lamps to electricity, to no avail. That's because utility poles in Glen Ridge run behind houses, through the backyards in a town where 85 percent of the homes are in a historic district.

"One of the things that define our streetscape is the lack of utility poles in the front yards, so there are no electric feeds from the road," said Michael Zichelli, the deputy borough manager. "We would have to get easements to run through their property and then run feeds from lamp to lamp." Too cost-prohibitive, he said.

So in the ensuing years, Glen Ridge — like one of its Essex County neighbors, South Orange — stood fast as the New York suburban holdouts. Of late, it hasn't been easy.

"Like everything that involves gas and energy, it's going up," said William Calabrese, who as South Orange's village president is the equivalent of the mayor.

Since 2002, the cost of running South Orange's 1,900 gaslights has surged 43 percent, with $860,000 now allocated in the 2006 budget — a $100,000 spike in just one year, according to the village executive's office.

In tiny Glen Ridge, though, where the average property-tax bill of $13,050 a year tops South Orange's by $1,500, Zichelli, the deputy borough manager, has been on a quest to make the lamps more cost-efficient.

To do that, he'd have to find a device that would automatically throttle down or shut the lamps off during the day, as was done long ago by ladder-climbing workmen who each week manually set their mechanical timers to extinguish them at night, ignite them at dusk.

The labor-intensive method, considered too costly, was abandoned some two decades ago, leading to what are now the equivalent of eternal flames.

"I was coming up empty," Zichelli said of his search.

It's a sentiment apparently shared by Robert Taylor, the manager of pricing at Public Service Electric & Gas, which actually owns and maintains the lamps and collects a tariff set by the New Jersey Board of Public Utilities.

"As of yet, we haven't found the technology to do it," he said.

But Michael Rohal, who as Glen Ridge's borough manager has to crunch the budget numbers each year, turned up a small Minnesota company called Knightronix, which for $225 a lamp says it can fit them with sensors that can turn them off during the day.

"We'd like to try a pilot with one or two lamps to determine their effectiveness," Rohal said.

Andy Knight, the Minnesota company's president, said the devices come with sensors to flag any malfunction with the so-called mantles, the illuminated part of the lamp that can become brittle if constantly subjected to the temperature extremes of being turned off and turned on. And Knight said there are mantles that can withstand the temperature swings.

Still, PSE&G said it has looked into Knightronix's product, concluding it would not be cost-effective when installation and maintenance costs are tallied. With so few gaslights in use today, the marketplace isn't producing alternatives. "There's not people knocking down our doors to market us technology," PSE&G's Taylor said.

Then there is the prospect of retrofitting Glen Ridge's 667-odd gaslights, a hodgepodge collection that includes long-ago discards from the New York City of a century ago. "The mechanics are a little different in every head," Zichelli said.

Should Glen Ridge convince PSE&G that the remedy works and is cost-effective, though, it could seek a lower tariff and cut its gaslight costs, conceivably in half. PSE&G's Taylor wasn't opposed to the idea.

"We would probably file something with the board (of public utilities) for a change in the rate," Taylor said.

A woman strolls past the Sunset Family Restaurant on Little Falls' reinvigorated Main Street. Run date, March 5, 2006.

36

MONTCLAIR: THEY LOVE IT BUT LEAVE IT
For many, lower taxes right next store

Just over the northwest border of Montclair, there's the little community of Little Falls, which always has been seen as a world away from its exclusive, nationally known neighbor.

But that is changing.

The former Passaic River mill town has become a home away from home for its share of Montclair expatriates. And why not? Most of Montclair State University is actually in Little Falls. So is the Yogi Berra stadium and museum, even though the former Yankee great's name long has been synonymous with Montclair.

For a number of Montclairions, Little Falls offers two big things: lower property taxes and a chance to downsize without losing proximity to Montclair stores and restaurants.

"The reason people are going to Little Falls is taxes: capital T, capital A, capital X, capital E, capital S. That explains it," said Carol Rhodes of Rhodes, Van Note Realtors in Montclair.

Ted Lippincott was lured by a condo at The Mill abutting the raging current of the Passaic River, after spending a good quarter-century moving into and updating large homes on Montclair's impressive Upper Mountain

Avenue.

When the moving bug struck again, he decided to downsize.

"I was sitting in my living room one evening and thinking, 'What do I need this for?'" said Lippincott, who is single. "I was certainly not going to do it again."

That was five years ago.

"There's quite a few of us (in Little Falls)," said Lippincott, who maintains strong ties with this old hometown and remains chairman of the Montclair Historic Preservation Commission.

Not far from Lippincott in Little Falls is Elizabeth Bartlett, the current president of the Montclair Women's Republican Club. Bartlett's reasons for leaving Montclair and her home on Melrose Place, though, differ from Lippincott's.

In a town where 79 percent of the electorate went for Democrat John Kerry in the last presidential election, she was feeling a little out of place. "I think there might be three Republicans in Montclair," she said.

She tells a tale of being stopped by a traffic light in Montclair while driving "a tacky car" with a lot of old bumper stickers when a reporter appeared at her window.

"I roll it down, and she said, 'I'm looking for a Republican. Here's my card. Give me a call.' That's a true story," Bartlett said.

But Little Falls had a pull of its own for Bartlett and her husband.

"A lot of lovely little streets with smaller houses on them," she said. "And that was very appealing to us — and, of course, the taxes."

In 2004 (the last data available), the average house in Montclair sold for nearly $480,000, while Little Falls prices averaged $326,500. The average property tax bill in Little Falls in 2004 was $5,671. In Montclair, it was $12,356. That $557-a-month savings could put a new luxury SUV in the driveway.

Still, Eugene Kulick, Little Falls' mayor, says there's much more to his town of almost 12,000, whose population is less than a third of Montclair's. There's the Historic Morris Canal Preserve, a pathway just off Main Street, and the train station packed with New York-bound commuters. There's the new classical town hall, which one envious former Montclair mayor once likened to "the halls of Congress," and the new restaurants, such as "381 Main," a popular martini bar.

To Kulick, Montclair spillover has had an effect. "People ran right to the bank and started fixing up their houses," he said. "It's a blue-collar town. Now, we've gotten a little upscale."

It hasn't gone unnoticed by real estate agents with deep Montclair roots.

In Little Falls, "Main Street has really rejuvenated in the past few years," said Linda Grotenstein of Coldwell Banker's Upper Montclair office. "Nice restaurants. Cute shops. And that's really happened recently."

Just along Main Street, the shops run the gamut from "The Pampered Pooch" to "Big Daddy's Sabrett Pushcart Hot Dogs." Next to Doug Belfondo's "Little Falls Health Foods" is a new arrival with a "grand opening" banner.

"The sushi place just opened a couple days ago," Belfondo said.

For families, the campus of Passaic Valley Regional High School, the "Home of the Hornets," is on Little Falls' East Main Street. There, the average SAT score is 975, versus 1083 at Montclair High, and 79 percent intend to go on to college, versus 81 percent in Montclair, but the average class size is smaller.

Back at The Mill, the two-bedroom, two-bath condos are billed as the "commuters' dream," with one now advertised as having 19-foot ceilings with exposed brick. It's listed at $394,000. The taxes: $4,900.

"It's that New York studio feel with the view of the falls," Vince Federico of Century 21 Van Der Wende Associates in Little Falls said of the development.

Lippincott will tell you he's in another world. "From where I'm sitting on the deck, you could be in Pennsylvania," he said. "You have no idea that Route 46 is in one direction and Willowbrook Mall is in another."

Yet like Lippincott, Penni Hayes maintains her Montclair connections some five years after her move to Little Falls. "I still attend Union Congregational Church in Upper Montclair," she said. "It's a matter of three miles from door to door. My activities have not changed."

Not that she isn't contributing to her new hometown.

"I helped them pay for the town clock," she said of her volunteer role in Little Falls. She, too, likes the classic Little Falls town hall, home to that classic clock.

"Oh. It's beautiful. It's beautiful."

Many luminaries lay at rest in Rosedale Cemetery, including former Gov. Charles Edison, son of inventor Thomas Edison, in this mausoleum. Run date, Dec. 2, 2005.

37

LIMITED ON SPACE BUT OPEN TO NEW IDEAS
Rosedale Cemetery is 165 years old

The titans of the pharmaceutical industry — Merck, Johnson, Upjohn — are buried here. So too is Thomas Edison's son and Samuel Colgate, founder of Colgate-Palmolive. It's also the final resting place of Andrew J. Eken, who brought the world the Empire State Building.

Yet Rosedale Cemetery, now marking its 165th anniversary, isn't resting on its laurels. It's a new century, after all, and this is a business, albeit a nonprofit one.

"This is the master plan," Robert Gist, who as the cemetery's general manager is the equivalent of the CEO, said as he scanned a wall-mounted artist's rendering of the outdoor columbarium that will — someday — hold the remains of at least 2,400.

"As we sell, we will add the number of units," Gist said of the columbarium with three sections of 824 "niche" spaces, each capable of ultimately holding two or three urns.

Home to some 60,000 of the dearly departed, Rosedale has limited space, like so many of the nation's older burial grounds, this one covering 92 acres in Montclair, Orange and West Orange.

"We're good for another 25, 30 years for interments," Gist said while showing off the designs and the cemetery's new "witnessing room" and "scattering area."

The updates are about as dramatic as the widespread introduction of crematories in the 1950s, when Rosedale's was built, and come in an era of storefront coffin shops, funeral concierge services and video-playing tombstones with solar-powered screens.

"They're forward-looking," Gist said of the elected board of trustees that has signed off on the updates at the nonsectarian cemetery.

It was just 11 months ago when funeral directors were invited to a "grand opening" of the witnessing room, designed to permit family to observe the start of the cremation process in private.

With five rows of stadium seating, it could pass for a entrepreneur's home theater. There, the push of a button on a black remote opens a curtain to a wide glass window, through which family can see the coffin of their loved one wheeled into a cremation chamber known as a retort.

Next to the window, there's an "override" switch, allowing, in the case of families of Asian-Indian descent, the oldest son to start the cremation process, Gist said. "It's part of their tradition," he said. "This gives the family peace of mind."

Just beyond Rosedale's main office and chapel lies the "scattering area," opened about three years ago. Wood chips are piled high. But a barren tree catches Gist's eye. "We lost an evergreen. All of a sudden, it just ...." He pauses and snaps his fingers. "Boom."

But new life, in the form of flowers and planters, he said, has yet to be added.

The grounds are a lure for the environmentally sensitive, Gist surmises. "I guess they just like nature more than anything else," he said. "We don't recommend. We just offer selection."

That's what is driving the "modern" cemetery, born of a change in American attitudes toward burial.

"More and more people have accepted cremation," said John Dodgson, who sits on the board of directors of the New Jersey Cemetery Association. "It allows them to personalize and actually witness the retort. It kind of adds to the closure for them."

Dodgson manages Ocean County Memorial Park in Toms River, a 100-acre cemetery founded in 1965. Its Web site, unlike Rosedale's, enables the bereaved to take virtual tours of the columbariums, zooming in on the inscriptions and even checking on the flowers from afar.

"A lot of families find comfort to see their mom's or dad's building from California or Colorado," Dodgson said of a Web site that also posts individual obituaries indexed by name.

But what Rosedale might lack in technology, it makes up for in sheer history — old and new.

Driving the grounds one day in his Mercury Mountaineer, Gist recalls that Stevie Wonder sang at a graveside service at Rosedale not long ago.

Nicole Kidman, he said, walked the grounds during shooting for the 2004 film "Birth," in which she plays Anna, a woman who believes her dead husband has come back in the form of a 10-year-old boy.

Gist has dealt with the tourist trade.

Every other year, busloads of Japanese citizens arrive to visit the graveside of James C. Hepburn, who died in 1911, but not before translating the Bible into Japanese. In 1987, his admirers erected a polished black granite monument bearing his likeness.

"It's constantly evolving," Gist said of the introduction of pictures, etched and otherwise, on tombstones.

The cemetery's lineage — detailed in a visitor's guide — also includes such notables as Althea Gibson, the tennis star who became the first African-American to win at Wimbledon, and Lowell Mason, a famous hymn writer who penned "Nearer My God to Thee."

Back at the main office, just beyond the counter with the well-worn black books bearing the cemetery maps, the radio at one point is playing the now timeless Beach Boys classic, "Surfin' Safari," remembered by a Baby Boom generation now nearing retirement.

Next to the rendering of the outdoor columbarium is one of the Glen Section, a 1,600-grave site just about to open for traditional interments. After that, just two sections remain, he said.

"But that doesn't mean interments will stop," said Gist, noting the abundance of family plots with unoccupied spaces.

The successive generations of New Jersey's pharmaceutical titans still visit, he said. So too does the Hartford family, descendants of George Huntington Hartford, the founder of A&P food stores who died in 1917.

One of the cemetery's most striking mausoleums, though, is drawing interest from non-relatives, namely funeral directors impressed with its oval top and stained-glass windows bearing biblical scenes.

Inside its heavy doors is a statue of a grieving young man, kneeling, his hand stretched across his face. It was constructed in 1916, according to cemetery records, for Otto Jaeger, who was listed as living on Montclair's Prospect Terrace and who was apparently the owner of the Paterson Plush Mills.

"They'd like to use the mausoleum," said Gist, suggesting the remains could be re-interred elsewhere if a family member were found and persuaded to do so. "It would (cost) a lot to build something like that today."

Gist, now 58, arrived at Rosedale in 1988, embarking on a second career after many years in government, most recently as Maplewood's town clerk. Here, he oversees a staff of eight full-timers and one part-timer. The grass-cutting and leaf-collecting, he said, are outsourced.

Should he ever leave, it's a place he'll ultimately be drawn back to. "My family's interred here," he said.

Asked if he'll follow, he said: "Looks that way. I'd have to say so."

Joyce Pisani, president of the North Caldwell Historical Society, walks in front of a cell at the old Essex penitentiary. Photo by Mitsu Yasukawa. Run date, April 20, 2007.

38

ONE LAST LOOK AT LIFE ON THE INSIDE
Tours of historic jail mark end of an era

In one of the darkened alleyways in the belly of the imposing brownstone tower of the old Essex County Penitentiary are the hieroglyphics of a lost culture.

Etched on one heavy door are the letters "ubnjail." A few inches away is one prisoner's undying denial: "I didn't do it. I was framed."

There are old cellblocks where one prisoner hung himself on Christmas Eve 1877, the tear gas canisters mounted in the old chapel, the shotgun portals in the main hall where prisoners sat behind glass to chat with visitors. All are revealing their secrets one last time.

"Can't you just feel the stories that the place has to tell?" asked historian Robert Williams, lugging an old jailer's set of keys as he leads a tour of an institution as noteworthy to some as San Francisco's Alcatraz.

The old jail high atop a hill in suburban North Caldwell is to fall to a wrecker's claw in the coming weeks, and with it the brownstone-and-mortar story of a self-sustaining prison work farm for petty criminals.

"It's really sad, because it's a beautiful, historic structure," said Williams, who can trace his family's roots in neighboring Verona to 1680 and is that town's historian.

In 2004, the "dungeonlike" jail annex with a record of mess-hall riots and escapes was sold as part of the vast Hilltop acreage to K. Hovnanian Cos., which is to build a 108-unit active-adult community called Four Seasons at North Caldwell.

Before it is razed, the public will have a opportunity to tour the jail this weekend. The North Caldwell Historical Society will conduct four tours to raise funds to help restore many of the artifacts, ledgers and documents recovered from the penitentiary.

As he has done many times, Williams yesterday walked through the jail, littered with everything from decades-old prisoner records to overturned pool tables in the chapel-turned-game room.

In the tower room, which dates to 1873, he points to the original square-head nails as well as names carved into the rafters, the oldest naming Andy Garry and dating to 1882. On the floor are tattered pay records and gasoline requisition slips from the mid-1930s.

At one point, Williams slips his arm through a door's broken pane and pulls out an "Inmate Handbook" from the era of Peter Shapiro, who served as county executive more than two decades ago.

"We'll give these out as souvenirs," he said of this weekend's tours.

The flashlight-carrying Williams soon steps into the "west wing," whose three stories have some 90 cellblocks, and tells of William Jones. In the 1870s, the prisoner, blind in one eye, refused to work in one of the prison's two quarries, fearing he'd loss the sight in his remaining eye from rock splinters. He was put in solitary confinement.

"He was bound and gagged. He ended up committing suicide on Christmas Eve, hung himself in one of the cells," he said while motioning down the long line of prison bars.

In the women's wing, built in 1915, Williams picks up orange prisoner garb with a large "P" for prisoner on the back. Rooms are ankle deep with decades-old files on inmates. "Adultery was a big one in the 1920s," Williams said.

In one manila file brown with age is the fingerprint card of a 38-year-old Newark woman whose 1938 arrest for "soliciting" got her six months at the penitentiary.

In another are records from 1942 detailing the case of a 35-year-old Newark man sentenced to a year for non-support of his three school-age children.

The file on the plumber, who had an arrest record for assault and battery against his wife, contains his commitment papers and cards detailing his mail and visitors. They included not only his sister, employer and mother, but also his spouse.

By August 1954, when the lockup held some 534 inmates, the jail made news with a new cafeteria deemed among the most modern in the nation. One of its distinguishing features: a little bulletproof-glass-encased tower where a guard carrying a tommy-gun stood watch.

The jail made headlines again in 1966, when a pre-Thanksgiving melee in the dining hall left three guards and 31 convicts injured in a hail of aluminum cups and flying utensils. It could have been worse. "We have an automatic tear gas set-up in the mess hall, but we didn't have to use it," the warden said at the time.

The cause of the riot was attributed to everything from the lack of dessert choices to the punishment of an inmate for stealing another prisoner's chocolate bar.

It wasn't all grim, however.

Just days before Christmas 1961, 22 men serving time for such offenses as drunkenness and vagrancy were set free in a show of leniency by a magistrate.

In 1964, again just before the holidays, about 30 prisoners entertained for relatives in an evening at "Cafe Escopen," which stood for Essex County Penitentiary. The backup talent included such volunteer guests as Bud Iannone of the Charlie Spivak Orchestra and Joe Dee, the musical director of the Meadowbrook Theater, according to press reports.

Today, the stage remains in a cavernous room with tear-gas canisters mounted on the walls and gun portals visible by the projection booth. A sign reads, "Capacity 298 sitting, 596 standing."

As for Williams, he has his own childhood memories of the orchards and chicken coops that dotted the penitentiary grounds. As a boy, he and friends once spotted a collectable glass insulator atop a telephone pole near "the prisoner's pond."

"We were thinking, 'How do we liberate this thing?'" he said. They spotted a group of prisoners and asked for help. "They discussed the whys and the wherefores and reported back a positive verdict," Williams said.

Then, a guard spotted the intrusion, leaving Williams with this memory: "Nice prisoners. The guard was mean."

Lucy Drago Benell is consoled by her husband, Michael, after serving her last lunch Friday at Lucy's Diner in Verona. Photo by Jon Naso. Run date, May 16, 2002.

39

IT'S CIAO TIME FOR A DINER OWNER
In Verona, they loved Lucy

It's been a while, but singer Connie Francis used to dine here. It seems appropriate since one of her biggest hits was "Where the Boys Are."

Lucy's Diner in Verona is where Lucy Drago Benell met her now husband, Michael, where co-owner Jack Drago met his longtime girlfriend, Marion Machucici, the self-proclaimed "Diner Queen."

Nuptials and near-nuptials aside, Lucy has sold her vintage 1950s diner after more than two decades of serving up Italian dishes within sight of Verona Park, in an eatery she purchased from Francis' father.

Births. Deaths. Marriages. She knew. Lucy was as much a fixture as the silvery walls, the grill with its sizzling ham and eggs.

"Huge portions," said one regular, a thin line of smoke rising from the cigarette in his ashtray.

His name?

"Lou, just Lou," he said, before reminiscing about what was.

"Kinda sad," he said yesterday, perched on one of the dozen stools as new owner Paraskevas "Paris" Vrouvas manned the grill as a cross-section of blue-collar and white collar New Jersey sat at the counter. Outside, a Lexus was parked aside a Ford truck.

"A wonderful woman," Lou said of Lucy.

"There was a regular crowd that came here morning and night. . . . Clair stayed on. She knows us by name," he said of longtime waitress Clair Mendel. "Lucy knew us by nicknames."

Before long, Lou is on his way. "Clair. I had a roll and coffee. $1.30."

"Thank you, Louie," she said. "See you later, sweetie."

It's exchanges like those that are forever cemented in Lucy's mind.

"That's the thing I'm going to miss the most," said Lucy, the Italian-born girl who last Friday spent her last working day at the diner, located on Lakeside Place, at the corner of Bloomfield Avenue. "They weren't customers. They were just good friends, very good friends."

Lucy, by all accounts, has a big heart. That's why she worked beyond the 7:30 p.m. closing time more than a few times. "I haven't had the heart to say to somebody, "I'm closing.' I didn't care if I had to work an extra hour a night."

And there were the eats. "The sauce is homemade. The cheese is so fresh," said Machucici, whose love of coffee, "great coffee" she'd say, helped bring her to Lucy's and led to her chance meeting with Lucy's brother and co-owner. "I always say the 'Diner Queen' met her king."

Lucy is well aware of the diner's romantic pairings.

"A lot of people met there," she said, laughing. "Some of them get married. Some of them get broken up."

But Machucici knows the work could be hard.

"They worked like dogs there. . . . I'm happy for them. I'm still the beneficiary of what they make because they are such great cooks."

Yesterday, news of Lucy's departure was still just that, news. A customer with shiny gray hair takes a seat at the counter and notices something amiss. "I haven't been here in a long time. She go back to Italy?" he asked.

"She retired," someone replied.

Well, not exactly.

On Tuesday, she admitted to doing a little shopping. The leisure time wasn't bad either. "It was kind of nice just to get up and work about in the house. Her husband, she said, is supportive.

"He figures, 'Lucy, you have more time for yourself. He said, 'Take it easy for a little while." No more need to remember everyone's order since she didn't write out counter checks, as diner folklore has it.

Customer Tom Kelch gets a strawberry sundae from Jack O'Neil, whose daughter, Linda Hofmann, owns Towne Scoop in Verona. Photo by Jim Pathe. Run date, June 8, 2008.

40

'AWFUL' LOT OF MEMORIES
New parlor drips with nostalgia

There's the towering plastic "Awful Awful" glass, with a little sign reading "TIPS" next to the cash register. The big wood sign on the wall reads "BOND'S ICE CREAM, Will Suit You to a `T.'"

Behind the counter is Jack O'Neil, wearing a white shirt and about to don a spiffy, though decades-old, black bow-tie. He's the guy who — from 1961 to 1969 — was behind the counter of his very own Bond's Ice Cream in Verona, one of a half-dozen parlors now the stuff of New Jersey legend.

The now 77-year-old counter man with piercing blue eyes drips with as much nostalgia as an ice cream cone on a hot day in his daughter's little ice cream shop.

"Everybody is happy that Bond's is back," said daughter Linda Hofmann, who with her husband, Bob, quietly opened what's really called the Towne Scoop about three weeks ago on Verona's Park Place.

The new shop has 16 flavors of ice cream — one more than the old

Bond's — and an assortment of ices, as well as shakes. "We have the big ones," O'Neil said of the shakes. "It's big, thick, just like it was. But we can't say, `Awful.'"(Newport Creamery, a Rhode Island company, secured the rights to the Awful Awful name when Bond's folded in the early 1970s and uses it to this day in more than a dozen stores in New England.)

O'Neil — and his young family — was at the helm of Bond's Ice Cream in Verona in an age when Ring Dings and Devil Dogs were sold in wax envelopes for a nickel.

Bond's Ice Cream was a destination. In addition to O'Neil's parlor in Verona, there were ones in Montclair, Cedar Grove, Clifton's Styertowne Shopping Center, Elizabeth and Short Hills.

The children of the Baby Boom generation plopped down at the stools for the ultimate challenge: drink a few "Awful Awfuls" and get one free. The framed Bond's menus on the walls of the Towne Scoop can jog a lot of memories.

"Awful Awful. It's a drink! 40 cents," reads one. The "Bond's Hamburger on toasted roll" could be had for 40 cents, too.

The memory of the ice cream parlors is so cemented in the local culture that just last year, a dedication brass tablet with an "Awful Awful" relief was erected on the site of the original Bond's — on Valley Road in Upper Montclair Village, where the Bank of America is today.

"Site of BOND'S, 1952-1973," it reads. "Home of the Awful Awful. Awful Big. Awful Good. Awful Lot of Memories."

The event, engineered by Montclair High's Class of '66, attracted Bond family members from as far away as Texas to mark an ice cream icon whose run lasted from 1934 to 1973.

One of those was Kathy Bond Borie, who came from her Vermont home to honor the family business begun by her grandparents, George and Bertha Bond. "There were three generations there," she said. "It was amazing to have all that celebration."

She, too, had an interest in O'Neil's memorabilia.

"Does he have a `Guzzler's Club' sign?" she said of the honor for those who could down three Awful Awfuls and get their names on the roster.

That milkshake feat also came with the awarding of a pin. "`I Was a Pig at Bond's," she said of the inscription. "I think one of my sisters has one."

The flashback to the Bond's of the 1960s doesn't end at the menu and signs in the Towne Scoop.

There is a framed black-and-white photograph, taken in 1966, of the O'Neil clan, sons Jack and Harold and daughter Linda. They're posed on the back of the elder O'Neil's 1924 Model T Huckster, with the inscription "Bond's Ice Cream, Worth Driving For, Verona, NJ."

He still has the Model-T. The photograph dated 2008 has the now-grown children taking the same pose as in 1966, with a little picture of Heather, who wasn't born yet in 1966, tucked in the corner.

O'Neil likes to reminisce about those long days at Bond's.

"That's Jack," O'Neil said while pointing to a picture of his one-time preschooler waxing the floor inside the old Bond's. "There he is making a banana split."

Daughter Linda Hofmann has a more up-to-date story.

"He comes in every morning and waxes the floor with that same waxer," she said of her father.

"Got to keep it clean," he replied.

The Towne Scoop — where a regular soft cone is $2.25 — is something of an extension of The Towne Store that Hofmann opened a year ago, hawking hometown apparel and such accessories as tie-dyed backpacks prominently stamped with "Verona."

That pride has seeped into the ice-cream parlor, with its checkered maroon and white floor tiles. "All Verona colors," she said.

These days, the young Jack pictured as a preschooler at Bond's is 46 and runs the nearby Lakeside Deli. His long-ago memories of Bond's are faint.

"I kind of remember it, not like I wish I did, since everyone says it was a heck of a place," he said.

On the wall of the Towne Scoop are framed pieces of American currency, a testament to a business's first customers, ahead of the grand opening. One of them belonged to John Terzo, a 27-year-old who runs the nearby JT's Barber Shop, with its rotating red, white and blue barber pole topped with a big white ball lamp.

"That's what it's all about," he said of the new ice cream parlor with the old memories. "It's all about not forgetting where you came from."

Diane Lubrano shares memories and laughs with her regular breakfast customers at the Cedar Grove Deli. Photo by Mia Song. Run date, March 30, 2008.

41

TODAY'S SPECIAL: MEMORIES OVER EASY
Cedar Grove celebrating centennial

The doors open at 6 a.m. at John Lubrano's little lunch counter, letting in old-timers who slip onto the four upholstered stools and use their hands to signal orders to the familiar waitresses.

"This is Mr. Cedar Grove," regular Bob O'Connell announces when Vince Pellegrino rushes in and unleashes a rat-tat-tat of small talk.

"This place is like Cheers — for breakfast," says Pellegrino, invoking memories of the old sit-com set in a Boston pub where "everybody knows your name."

The memories run deep at the Cedar Grove Deli, smack in the center of a little town that is in the midst of celebrating its centennial under the slogan "A Century of Memories."

Diane Lubrano, standing behind the counter where the wall-mounted menu touts "Rise and Shine Breakfast" selections, knows the regulars well. "This is a local place," she said of the narrow eatery with historic photographs lining the walls over the few booths.

Here, the customers glance out on their stretch of the Newark-Pompton Turnpike that decades ago was the semirural trail to Frank Dailey's Meadowbrook, the big-band roadhouse that hosted the likes of the Dorsey

Brothers and singer Kitty Kallen.

"The best description of this is like going to the general store, standing by the potbellied stove," O'Connell said of the chatter.

All seem to have some connection to the old Frank Dailey's Meadowbrook, whose big-band years died off in the 1950s and whose revivals included stints as a dinner-theater and later a disco and teen dance hall.

"I used to work there, washing dishes," said Dan Pacifico, who was a high school student in Montclair who got glimpses of the Dorsey band and Sammy Kaye during the mid-1940s.

"He spent the war at the Meadowbrook," O'Connell chimes in.

In the 1960s, O'Connell used to ferry groups to see the likes of actresses Jane Russell and Shelley Winters performing at the Meadowbrook Dinner Theater. "I used to run bus trips to the Meadowbrook . . . senior citizen groups," he said. "I used to hustle trips."

On April 12, the old ballroom — remodeled as a church hall since being acquired by Sts. Kiril and Metodij Macedonian Orthodox Church — will be the site of the Centennial Ball.

James Reilly, a volunteer Cedar Grove firefighter, is going. So, too, are his brethren, he said after taking a seat at the counter with his 13-year-old son, James Michael Reilly.

"It's like our firemen's night out," he said. "Twenty firefighters. I think two people are bringing their wives."

Cedar Grove, a Republican-leaning town of some 12,800 people tucked into some 4.5 square miles, has chalked up a lengthy résumé since its founding on April 9, 1908, after spending a time as a piece of neighboring Verona.

One of its own, Arthur Wynne, is credited with inventing the crossword puzzle. Allen B. DuMont, a pioneer in development of television, once experimented in his own Cedar Grove garage.

It is now the home of Philip Jaeger, who penned the pictorial history "Cedar Grove," distributed by Arcadia Publishing. He even acquired an original DuMont television on eBay. He's ready for the April 12 dinner gala and the nostalgic introduction once broadcast on the radio coast-to-coast.

"The lights will be dimmed and over the loudspeakers will come, `Coming to you from Frank Dailey's Meadowbrook on the Newark-Pompton Turnpike in Cedar Grove, New Jersey, we bring you . . .,'" he said.

The memories are being stirred up, too, at www.cedargrovenj.org, which is linked to online pages with information on everything from

Centennial Ball tickets, available for purchase now through April 7, and the June 28 parade and picnic.

Today, Cedar Grove is home to such notables as Michael Uslan, the executive producer of the highly successful Batman movies, and Tommy James, who once topped the charts as the lead of Tommy James & the Shondells.

"He lives up there?" waitress Diane Ryan said after learning that Pellegrino resides in the same neighborhood as the 1960s pop icon. Then she blurted out the group's big hit of 1967, "I Think We're Alone Now."

As for Diane Lubrano, it is her son, John, who runs the Cedar Grove Deli. But they got their start across the street at the family business, Poppa Tony's, which had a 30-year run starting in 1971 and lives on in the menu.

The "Poppa Tony's Specialties" include the famed tomato Alfredo soup, which is still a big draw around the holidays when families come in to cart away 32-ounce containers of the concoction.

A couple of doors down, Lucille DeFranza mans the counter at the Treasures Unlimited jewelry store. She, too, can be found popping in at the Cedar Grove Deli.

She recalls accompanying a young man from Newark's Central High School to his prom at The Meadowbrook. There were other forays as well, even to see an up-and-coming singer appearing with the Dorsey band. His name was Frank Sinatra.

"We saw him," she said. "Very skinny."

The Friar Tuck Inn opened along Pompton Turnpike in Cedar Grove in 1952. Run date, Nov. 27, 2005.

42

THE FRIAR TUCK'S CLOSING CHAPTER
Longtime restaurant sold in Cedar Grove

The dining rooms carried such names as Camelot, Nottingham and Sussex. On the menu, there was Will Scarlet's catch and Maid Marion's black forest cake.

In 1952, Francis "Jake" Jacobs opened his Friar Tuck Inn along Cedar Grove's Pompton Turnpike, not far from the famed Frank Dailey's Meadowbrook. But first, the tavern's old moniker - the Dutch House - and its accompanying theme had to go.

"They lassoed the windmill that was at the top of the Dutch House and pulled it down," said Philip Jaegar, a Cedar Grove historian who heard the story from Jacobs not long before the innkeeper's death in 2003.

Now it's the Friar Tuck's turn.

It's a bittersweet moment for Jennifer Wells, Jacobs' 50-something daughter, who sold the Friar Tuck and simultaneously ended a family tradition that began when her great-grandmother, Annie Jacobs, opened the Robin Hood Inn in Clifton in 1913.

"To really take it to the next level, it would need a huge investment," she said of the reasons for selling the inn to new owners who intend to erect a modern catering hall. "At this stage in our lives . . . the only guarantee would be that we work twice as hard."

She had already rung up untold hours at the Friar Tuck, starting as a preschooler.

"My father taught me how to count on the liquor bottles," Wells said of those days her father took inventory and threw in a little arithmetic. "Take one bottle away, and what's left?"

It was the start of a lifetime of memories. "You name it. I did it all, except cook," she said.

Reunions. Retirements. Marriages. The Friar Tuck saw it all.

"I remember my parents took me there as a kid for Sunday afternoon brunch," said Thomas Tucci, who today is Cedar Grove's township manager. "It's a landmark, similar to the Meadowbrook."

The tie-in with the Meadowbrook, a Big Band venue, has some folklore of its own.

As Wells heard it, the song "Down the Road Apiece" - the Don Raye tune recorded in 1941 by the Will Bradley-Ray McKinley Orchestra and subsequently recorded by the Rolling Stones - was about the Friar Tuck's original 1938 building.

"It was a place to hang out after they were done with their gigs at the Meadowbrook," she said.

Wells, too, can rattle off some of the luminaries who've had brushes with the Friar Tuck.

There was Dorothy Lamour, the actress perhaps best-known for playing opposite Bob Hope and Bing Crosby in the "Road" movie series, including "Road to Singapore," "Road to Zanzibar" and "Road to Morocco"; Buzz Aldrin, the man who stepped on the moon just moments after Neil Armstrong in 1969; and Yankee greats Yogi Berra of Montclair and Phil Rizzuto of Hillside.

"Bill Bradley, of course," she said of the former New York Knicks star who became a U.S. senator and a candidate for the Democratic presidential nomination.

And those countless reunions. One of the last was Montclair High's Class of 1959. Marge and Bob Mac Lachlan, who now live in Liberty Township, remember last October's as just one of a lifetime of memorable moments at the inn.

"We've been there so many, many times," Marge Mac Lachlan said. "Our parents had been there. You like to follow through on that. It gives you a sense of belonging."

How the Friar Tuck got its name is not entirely clear.

The Dutch House restaurant was built in 1938, the same year "The Adventures of Robin Hood" premiered with Errol Flynn as Robin and Eugene Pallette as Friar Tuck. The flick had a healthy run in a re-release in the late 1940s, not long before Jacobs bought the place.

"My dad just carried on the tradition," she said of the Friar Tuck's debut after the Robin Hood. "I have no idea why my great-grandmother decided on that (Robin Hood) name."

The inn's sale was handled by J.C. Kapas of Rochelle Park, which as "The Restaurant Specialists" has since 1963 handled the sales of such long-gone eateries as Gene Boyle's in Clifton.

Today the Friar Tuck seems suspended in time. Peer inside the gold-colored revolving glass door, and the green-leaf motif of the carpet looks fleshly crisp, the large copper tea kettle ready to provide a shot of caffeine.

"It seems like the new owners haven't even walked in since we left," Wells said.

But they've been around.

Like Jacobs before him, new owner Jimmy Vasilopoulos - the second generation of the family that has run Clifton's Tick Tock Diner on busy Route 3 West since 1987 - has a new vision for the Cedar Grove landmark. His Second Generation Catering Inc. paid $1.75 million for the property on July 1.

"We're looking to do a more upscale place, something more luxurious . . . possibly tear it down or expand it. We're not sure yet," Vasilopoulos said.

The new catering hall - at 70,000 square feet, more than twice as large as the Friar Tuck - does not yet have a name, but Vasilopoulos hopes to start work in the spring or summer. Before then, there might be the restaurant equivalent of an estate sale.

"We're probably going to do some type of auction," he said of the left-behinds that won't be put to use.

Even now, an old postcard of the Friar Tuck's cocktail lounge can he found on eBay, with a sale price of $7.99 set by the owner in Prescott, Ariz.

The original Dutch influence will remain, though. The sale of the inn and its 3.49 acres includes the Personette House, a Dutch farmhouse built in 1771 and marketed by the Friar Tuck as a desired locale for a bridal party's cocktail hour and photos.

Vasilopoulos, too, sees it as a spot for wedding photos and the like.

Joe Biglin, for one, won't soon forget the wedding reception he and his new bride, Sue, had at the Friar Tuck in 1984 before departing on a honeymoon in St. Lucia.

It was an easy choice. Biglin had worked there through his high school and college years. "Busboy, car-parker, waiter and bar tender," said Biglin, who now lives in Flanders.

And he remembers one of the inn's mainstays as a guy with thick eyeglasses who went by the name of "Chuck."

"He had these glasses that were so thick, he'd see a fork that was misplaced five tables away," Biglin said. "He was just amazing."

Producer Michael Uslan, left, filmmaker Chip Cronkite and cartoonist Joe Kubert during the filming of a documentary at Kubert's School of Cartoon and Graphic Art in Dover. Photo by Jerry McCrea. Run date, July 15, 2007.

43

THE MEN BEHIND THE MEN BEHIND THE MASKS
They're a portal to world of Pop! Zap! and Wham!

Michael Uslan ascends the stairs of his stately New Jersey home, leaving behind the stacks of Architectural Digests, the coffee table book "Rwanda Nziza" and the African masks on the wall.

In moments, the formal space that was his living room gives way to a new world populated by Batman, Captain Marvel and the Green Lantern.

Trailing Uslan — who sports a T-shirt stamped with the title of one of his many blockbuster Batman films —is Chip Cronkite, the son of famed broadcaster Walter Cronkite. He's toting a palm-sized Panasonic 4.0 mega pixel camera.

The stair-climb to Uslan's own personal bat cave was the start of a Cronkite documentary featuring interviews with the aging stars of comic-book land, ahead of an unparalleled exhibit at the Montclair Art Museum that opened yesterday.

"Hey Chip," Uslan says. "You want to come up into our toy store?"

His classic brick colonial is just a few miles from where "Reflecting

Culture: the Evolution of American Comic Book Superheros" just opened for a six-month run.

Inside is a world of Pow! Zap! and Wham!

His desk and bookshelf-lined walls are packed with everything from Batman lunchboxes and figurines from his "Constantine" film to his Emmy for TV's "Where on Earth is Carmen Sandiego?" and even a throwback to Hollywood's past, namely the black bird of 1941's "The Maltese Falcon."

This day, Uslan, whose résumé includes executive producer roles in 2005's "Batman Begins" and soon-to-be-released "The Dark Knight," is gathering up some of his personal collection, as archivists with blue surgical gloves, acid-free paper and bubble-wrap ready the pieces for shipment.

There's "Action Comics" No. 252, whose May 19, 1959, publication featured the first appearance of Supergirl, and 1956's "Showcase" No. 4, where the re-appear ance of Flash after a long absence is considered the dawn of the Silver Age of comics.

That cover was the handiwork of Joe Kubert.

"Before you sit, Joe, we'll light you up," Cronkite said about two weeks later, as his small production crew landed in the 80-year-old icon's office at the Joe Kubert School of Cartoon and Graphic Art in Dover.

Kubert is on a list of 19 creators — all in their 80s and 90s — who took the Uslan-Cronkite team coast-to-coast, a tour that included an interview on June 20 in Los Angeles with Stan Lee, co-creator of Spider-Man, X-Men and The Fan tastic Four, to name a few.

The relaxed-looking Kubert, wearing a blue short-sleeve button-down shirt and jeans, sits at his drawing table amid the colorful likes of Hawkman, Tarzan and Sgt. Rock.

Uslan and Cronkite, who first teamed up in 1985 for a PBS mini-series on the Salem Witch Trials, go to work. The sound man is quiet. So too is the cameraman. Cronkite is taking notes. Uslan is asking the questions.

"Did you know it was the Golden Age?" Uslan asks of Kubert's early years in comics, "Or was it about scratching out a living?"

Kubert, who is also tapping his personal collection for the Montclair exhibit, pauses.

"To me, the thing that motivated me to do this was my love of drawing," Kubert says. "The fact that I could make a buck on it was an added incentive."

Later, he notes that the "buck" was actually $5 — per page. "I made more money than my father made as a kosher butcher," he says.

As Cronkite shuffles his papers inside a glossy Montclair Art Museum folder, Uslan poses question after question, barely paying attention to his script. Kubert gives some sage advice.

"The best stories are character- driven," Kubert says.

Soon, Uslan notes that comics have been mainstreamed over the decades into an art form and into the halls of The Louvre in Paris and the Smithsonian Institution. Even more, Uslan says, they've become the main source of the biggest blockbuster movies of Hollywood.

"Amazing," Kubert says. He never would have believed it back in the 1940s, he says. "I´d laugh my head off."

Post-interview, Uslan says he has been transported back in time during what will become a one-hour documentary, clips of which will be shown at the Montclair exhibit. "That was amazing. I'm like 16 again."

Just a few days earlier, Uslan was taping the audio for the exhibition tour at the museum´s Le Brun Library, quoting the scripture of his world.

"Superman, who came to Earth with powers and abilities far beyond mortal men," says Uslan, repeating one of comic-dom´s most remembered lines.

But Uslan never overlooks the connection to mere mortals.

He tells the story of the Man of Steel, whose escape from the doomed planet Krypton mirrors Moses´ infant ride in a wicker basket down the Nile, and their subsequent roles as strangers in strange lands.

"Sound familiar?" Uslan says on the audio.

Of course, Uslan was one of the lucky ones who managed to hang on to those classic 12-cent comic books. Some years ago, he was going through boxes in his parents' home and opened up his "sixth grade box." Out fell three comics, including Kubert´s now rare "Showcase" No. 4.

"My Mom and Dad let me keep mine, and this was a treasure my son, David, and I found it in a garage in Montclair."

Glen Ridge policeman Chris Grogan, the first motorcycle patrolling officer in decades, lays in wait for drivers. Photo by Jerry McCrea. Run date, July 16, 2006.

44

TO CATCH A SPEEDING BULLET

A fully loaded Harley that's not just for parades

Christopher Grogan has traded in his "regular Crown Vic" patrol car for a shiny new black-and-white.

There's the full fenders, the big chrome headlight and a head-turning chassis. It's a Harley Road King, and Grogan is the first Glen Ridge patrolman to saddle one in decades.

The new Harley-Davidson is just back from the decal shop, and Grogan's just back from two weeks of grueling biker training. He's raced in simulated chases at Giants Stadium, swerved around 2-by-4 timbers thrown in his path, and crouched behind his Harley for cover from a hail of pink paint balls.

Good thing they weren't bullets. "There's not much coverage," the knee-high-boot-wearing Grogan said while standing next to his one-seater black-and-white in a coveted garage spot next to Glen Ridge Police Headquarters.

"I suppose you don't want to hide behind the gas tank," Police Chief John Magnier said with a grin.

It was Grogan, at age 33, who emerged from a field of a half-dozen motorcycle-cop wannabees to ride the "M1," a 900-pound one-seater soon to be 1,100 pounds when fully loaded with everything from a hand-held radar gun to a BlackBerry-like device that can run a license plate.

He was long ago primed for this moment.

This biking aficionado has a personal stable of two Aprilias and a single Suzuki at his Hawthorne home. "I'm down to three bikes," said a smiling Grogan, quick to offer an explanation. "I started riding dirt bikes when I was 5." It was a hand-me down from his uncle.

"It became an obsession," said Grogan, a one-time sheriff's officer less than a year into his stint at the Glen Ridge police.

The new Harley turned heads during its inaugural run at Glen Ridge's Memorial Day Parade. "They were shouting, `We got a bike?'" Grogan said of the remarks. "That's the beauty. You hear everything."

Glen Ridge, in fact, is among the latest departments to embrace motorcycles after a hiatus stretching in some cases back a half-century. "They are starting to make a comeback," Magnier said. Back in 1913, Glen Ridge's police force had one motorcycle, a full decade before it got its first patrol car. In 1954, motorcycles were phased out entirely.

At the New Jersey State Police, a pilot program returning motorcycles to law-and-order patrol for the first time in 30 years was just formalized in March, less than three years after it began.

The State Police had disbanded its motorcycle unit in 1954 after 17 troopers were killed in motorcycle accidents in the agency's first 30 years.

"Four and we're getting two more," State Police Sgt. Michael Ambrosio said of their biker ranks he heads up out of the Holmdel barracks on the Garden State Parkway.

They've had only minor injury, he said, when one biker dove off his motorcycle just before it was rear-ended. "The training is paramount," he said of avoiding accidents.

In Montclair, Police Chief David Sabagh swears by the fleet of three Harleys that sprung up there just a few years ago. "Going great," he said. "Our radar enforcement has been up 40 percent over the last two years. . . . They're great for parades and a great public relations tool."

As for Grogan, in just two weeks he's rung up 800 miles on his Harley, leased from Seacoast Harley-Davidson in North Hampton, N.H., in a pilot program Magnier said is costing less than $4,000 in its first year.

Nearly all the mileage — 600 miles in fact — was tallied at a Maryland State Police training course at the Bergen County Police Academy, where

Grogan graduated in the top of his 12-member class. Easy rider it wasn't.

He's swerved through maze after maze of yellow cones, kept his wits in a motorcycle "pack" formation and took fire in the paint ball attack.

"Officer survival," said Michael Grasso, a Cedar Grove motorcycle patrolman who was one of Grogan's instructors. "Just to show them how vulnerable they are and how minimal their coverage is."

"It's intimidating, but it's very real," said Grogan, who has earned his distinctive "flying wheel" arm patch. And those $200 knee-high boots. "It takes about an hour to shine each one," he said.

But ahh, that private parking space, next to the wall sign reading "HARLEY-DAVIDSON PARKING ONLY." It was a birthday gift from friends, he said, who knew he didn't have one, at least not yet.

"As a joke, they got me the sign," Grogan said. "I said, 'This is perfect!' It went right up."

Run date, Dec. 20, 2002

45

THE BIG PICTURE IN GLEN RIDGE

Neighbors get to do some star-gazing

Preppy-looking actors and actresses dotted the pews at the Glen Ridge Congregational Church, some napping amid loads of bags and coats during a break yesterday in filming for the movie "Mona Lisa Smile" starring Julia Roberts.

Yellow signs reading "S.A.G." - Screen Actors Guild - marked some of the pews, and the church doors bore such signs as "Extras Holding" and "Makeup and Costumes."

"It's a odd-looking gaggle of people here, isn't it?" said the Rev. J. David Stinson while passing a stack of name tags worn on Sundays by his parishioners. "I almost took an offering."

Hollywood came to Glen Ridge on Tuesday in a big way, and it was more than just the two-dozen trailers lining Ridgewood Avenue. This was a big budget production, and the money was flowing.

Stinson wouldn't pinpoint the monetary gain for his church, but he did offer a clue. "It's not going to solve all our problems," he said before pausing. "The movie company has been very generous."

At Glen Ridge Borough Hall, Borough Manager Michael Rohal rattled off some of the take, besides the $500-a-day fee the town collects and the $40-an-hour pay for each police officer on duty. The studio, he said, gave $2,500 to the high school for new lockers, $1,000 for the Southend Neighborhood Association and even $1,000 for last month's Ashenfelter 8K race, named for town resident Horace Ashenfelter, gold medalist in the steeplechase in the 1952 Helsinki Olympic Games.

"We appreciate it," Rohal said.

Outside the church stood a heated 50-by-100-foot tent, rented from Party Line Rentals of Elmsford, N.Y., with room for 500 diners. A memo-board menu next to a lighted Christmas tree showed some of the entrees: chicken fajitas, pesto pasta.

Around the corner by the church's side entrance, a "featured extra" by the name of Sean Reilly stood atop the steps from the basement dressing room, where extras prepared for the big dance scene.

Reilly plays a Harvard man in the film, a drama about a Wellesley

College art history teacher who inspires her students to challenge how they are expected to live.

"I get in most of the shots," Reilly said, explaining the significance of the term "featured." Two blocks away at the Women's Club of Glen Ridge, the big scene has been in the works for two days. Inside, under a "Spring Fling 1954" banner attached to a string of paper Chinese lanterns, there's the dance floor surrounded by round tables with lavender cloths.

The service tables feature large silver bowls with orange and lemon slices floating in the punch, round silver trays of sugar cookies and white napkins bearing the blue Wellesley insignia inscribed in Latin.

Walking by outside yesterday was Tami Kinley, pushing an empty two-seater stroller that moments before had been filled with presents she deposited at the post office.

"I knew I wasn't going to find parking," she said. "And I was hoping to catch a glimpse of Julia Roberts." Snapping pictures outside was Bob Chamberlin, who coincidentally has lived in Glen Ridge since 1954. He got some pictures of Roberts in October, when she and co-star Julia Stiles were doing a front porch scene on Douglas Road for "Mona Lisa Smile."

Chamberlin, who lives on Sherman Avenue, said the closest he came personally to a movie production was when a commercial for Life Savers was filmed 27 years ago at the house next door to him.

"Life Savers, Wow, Lemon. That was the tag on it," he said.

As for his picture-taking yesterday, Chamberlin said it was for posterity. "I like to record this just for the record and maybe to see Julia."

Ham radio enthusiast John Burgio, left, of North Caldwell, and Tom Christian, the ham radio "Voice of Pitcairn," finally met face-to-face after years of communicating via radio. Pitcairn is a South Pacific Island. Photo by Saed Hindash. Run date, June 30, 2002.

46

HAM OPERATOR MEETS A FARAWAY VOICE

It's a descendant linked to "Mutiny on the Bounty"

Tom Christian is the ham radio "Voice of Pitcairn."

Pitcairn is small piece of an archipelago in the middle of the South Pacific. It is one of the last outposts of the British Empire, a place inhabited by a mere 44 people who each year burn Capt. William Bligh in effigy.

Christian - the great-great-great-grandson of Fletcher Christian, the first mate who sent the tyrannical Capt. Bligh adrift in a 1789 insurrection immortalized in "Mutiny on the Bounty" - has just had his first face-to-face with another ham radio "voice."

He's John Burgio, the 81-year-old husband of a one-time New Jersey secretary of state who lives on North Caldwell's Mountain Avenue.

W2JB (that's Burgio), meet VP6TC (that's Christian).

"When you mention radio amateurs, you should always mention their call letters," said Burgio, who after a few decades of brief and often technical radio contacts finally saw Christian eye-to-eye, even put him up as a house guest. "My e-mail is W2JB," Burgio adds with enthusiastic pride.

In fact, call letters were everywhere as Burgio and about two-dozen of his brethren from the North Jersey DX Association had a decidedly American hot dog and hamburger cookout for their unusual guest late Thursday.

Among the parked cars near the front lawn tent is one bearing the vanity plate K2CO. Sitting close to Christian is a man with a baseball cap embroidered with the letters N2JD. All wear name tags bearing their call letters, with Burgio's wife, Jane, who was secretary of state in the Kean administration, wearing a name badge with the letters XYL atop John's call letters, a signal that she's a spouse.

A 110-foot radio tower rises skyward over the Cape Cod house. Warren Hager (he's K2UFM and the club's official cook) is just outside the tent, minding burgers over a small, round charcoal grill. "He's an easy guy to talk with, that man," he says of Christian, noting that the guest helped prepare the fruit medley. "You ought to see him cut up a pineapple."

In one folding chair in a circle of many sits Christian, biting into a cheeseburger.

"I find the American hams very hospitable," says Christian, who today will be flying to ancestor Fletcher Christian's birthplace, the Isle of Man in the United Kingdom, on an invitation to appear at a festival. "I'll have to hire a tuxedo suit, and I'm not looking forward to that."

Christian is a sought-after man. He remembers his first trip to America, as the "real Mr. Christian" in a 1967 segment of television's "To Tell the Truth." "I think I got about $125 for that, but it was fun."

But among hams, more specifically the long-distance DXers as they are called, he's treasured for another reason: a chance to get a QSL card from a tiny island with no regular phone service and big breaks in radio communication.

"Most DXers have shoeboxes of the cards," said Steven Adell, a club member from Roxbury. "They collect them like stamps." Get 100 and there's an award, a highly treasured certificate from the American Relay Radio League.

Urb LeJeune (he's W2DEC) is proud of his. "I have a card from Tom from 1957, when he was first licensed," says LeJeune, who later in the evening managed to get Christian to autograph one of the 50-cent Pitcairn postcards he sells at home and in his journeys.

Christian has brought with him a small supply of color T-shirts and caps, bearing pictures of the famous British ship and the lettering "HMS Bounty."

He has spoken to but never met Marlon Brando, who played Fletcher Christian in the 1962 film version of "Mutiny on the Bounty." He has had his share of Bounty questions - the most frequently asked - over the years. "It's too old," he says. "It's like me asking, 'What do you think of the Civil War?'"

Yet, at 66 and as the father of four grown daughters, he's mindful of his ancestry. "I'd like to be able to go to Tahiti and trace my ancestry with the women," he says of the native born who married many of the mutineers, "because no credit has been given to them really."

Christian's father was in his 20s when the elder Christian's grandfather, Thursday October Christian, died in his 90s in 1911, meaning there was time to pass original stories down. "My father told me so many things when I was young," Tom Christian says, "and I didn't pay enough attention."

For now, this descendant of a mutineer is among those he describes as the "worldwide brotherhood," at times raising medical help for those on the island and leading to honors as an MBE, Member of the British Empire.

It is a brotherhood that has afforded him the hospitality - and accommodations - of his New Jersey visit.

The night before in Burgio's basement radio room, Christian was able to e-mail his wife, Betty, via the island's satellite hookup, telling her of his journey.

Does e-mail threaten amateur radio? Burgio is asked.

"Absolutely," he says. "Young people at 16, 17 are becoming computer whizzes and missing out on this great hobby."

Elisabeth Shue, a South Orange native and an Oscar nominee for 1997's "Leaving Las Vegas," works on the set of the movie "Gracie" in Maplewood. Photo by Matt Rainey. Run date, Sept. 12, 2006.

47

ACTRESS HOME TO FILM '70S FLICK 'GRACIE'
Elisabeth Shue revisits her old haunts in Maplewood

Inside Village Trattoria, a pizzeria tucked on a side street in quaint Maplewood Village, the advertising poster hanging near the oven pictures a cooler full of Pepsi-Cola, not in aluminum cans but the old long-necked bottles.

"It's got a lot to give," proclaims the vintage 1970s sales pitch.

The booths are yellow Formica, chipped in places, their table tops dotted with Pepsi bottles and small white paper plates topped with slices of plain pizza. All are props.

Out steps Elisabeth Shue, known as "Lisa" to her friends.

"I was driving around," the actress and Oscar nominee for 1997's "Leaving Las Vegas," said of her old haunts. "Every little nook and cranny has a memory for me."

The blond-haired alumna of Maplewood's Columbia High School and the girl who back in the 1970s lived on South Orange's Meeker Street and later Turrell Avenue was back in her hometown digs yesterday for the feature film "Gracie."

Her husband, Davis Guggenheim — the director of "Gracie" who was most recently in the limelight for directing the Al Gore global-warming flick "An Inconvenient Truth" — laughed when asked about being in his wife's old stomping ground.

"I think it's very special, just our family coming and eating in all the places she used to eat," he said. "It's like a homecoming."

Set in 1978, "Gracie" — inspired by real-life events in the Shue family — is the story of a 16-year-old girl who, after a family tragedy, fought for and won the right for girls to play the competitive team sport of soccer.

The film, too, is something of a family affair.

"Gracie" includes Shue's real-life brothers Andrew, in a starring role, and John, on the business end. In the film, Elisabeth Shue's character is the mother of Gracie Bowen, played by 15-year-old Carly Schroeder, who last appeared with Harrison Ford in "Firewall."

Among her "Gracie" film family is Trevor Heins, a 12-year-old boy from Medford who played Connor in television's "Rescue Me" series but is now playing Shue's screen son, Daniel Bowen.

"She's really nice. I'd like to have her as a mom," the blond-haired, freckled-faced boy said while sitting next to his mother, Jackie, during lunch break on Maplewood's Inwood Place.

"He didn't eat much because he had pizza during the scene," she said of their lunch plans.

It was so much pizza, so little to eat, at least for Angelo and Mary Vayas, who as the owners of Village Trattoria prepared the pizza pies but couldn't eat the props. "You want to just go to the diner?" Mary Vayas said of the couple's lunch plans.

Moments earlier, Angelo Vayas was arranging tri-fold menus bearing the eatery's name in a wicker basket, positioning them so they might — just might — get captured on film.

What is more likely to get some free exposure is a large poster, by Maplewood artist David Heffernan, depicting the old Irvington-Maplewood playland Olympic Park, home to "the largest swimming pool in the East."

"That would be really neat," Mary Vayas said of the prospect.

Outside, by the vintage Mercury Cougar and Cadillac Fleetwood bearing 1978 New Jersey inspection stickers, there were corps of support staff, backed up by PAs, or production assistants.

Standing guard inside the "EXIT" door of the Bank of America was Martha Tuber of New York City, a plastic coffee cup sitting on the floor.

Her job: keeping bank customers from walking out the glass doors and getting in the shot while the film was rolling.

Her coffee cup as close as it was, she had been mistaken for a panhandler.

"Somebody thought I was asking for money," Tuber said.

Outside, another PA, sporting a green Puma cap and blue jeans fashionably ripped at the knee, was standing guard, along with a couple pairs of Maplewood's finest, wearing easy-to-spot yellow shirts.

"That's a cut," she yelled.

Soon, she struck up a conversation with Carlos Baez, one of the patrolmen.

"Are they doing the same scene over and over and over?" he said.

"Different camera angles" came part of the otherwise lengthy response.

As for Fred Profeta, Maplewood's mayor, the days of filming will give the small Essex County town national exposure. The town in the movie, in fact, is called Maplewood, and the high school where filming was conducted last week will carry the Columbia High School name in theaters, he said.

He has spoken to Andrew Shue, once a pro player with the Los Angeles Galaxy, about helping out in a capital campaign for a new soccer field. "He indicated he will play a role," he said.

Back in her high school days, Elisabeth Shue confessed, she ate her pizza around the corner at the Roman Gourmet, a 35-year-old mainstay abutting the Maplewood Theater.

"I loitered," she said of the place during her teen years.

There, Vinnie Loffredo, another generation in the family-run business, confirmed the Shue connection, saying his place was in business long before Village Trattoria opened.

"This is the place where she got pizza," he said. About 15 years ago, he said, she even returned for a cameo of sorts. "She picked up a pie. She picked it up herself."